Ed James

The game cock: being a practical treatise on breeding, rearing, training, feeding

The origin and cure of diseases, and the revised cocking rules governing all

parts. Second Edition

Ed James

The game cock: being a practical treatise on breeding, rearing, training, feeding
The origin and cure of diseases, and the revised cocking rules governing all parts.
Second Edition

ISBN/EAN: 9783337147020

Printed in Europe, USA, Canada, Australia, Japan

Cover: Foto ©Lupo / pixelio.de

More available books at **www.hansebooks.com**

THE
GAME COCK:

BEING A

PRACTICAL TREATISE

ON

BREEDING, REARING, TRAINING, FEEDING, TRIMMING, MAINS, HEELING, SPURS, ETC., ETC., ETC.

TOGETHER WITH AN

EXPOSURE OF COCKERS' TRICKS.

THE

ORIGIN AND CURE OF DISEASES,

AND THE REVISED

COCKING RULES

GOVERNING ALL PARTS OF THE WORLD

BY

ED. JAMES.

PUBLISHED BY

ED. JAMES, 88 AND 90 CENTRE STREET, N. Y

NEW YORK CLIPPER BUILDING.

1873.

Second Edition.

M. T. TYLER, Printer,
88 and 90 Centre street, New York.

PREFACE.

In the publication of this little work on the Game Cock, the compiler, from long experience as a sporting journalist, feels that he is giving to the breeders and fanciers of Games a book which they stand greatly in need of. It has been prepared with great care and attention to all the minor details, as well as the more important ones, and written so as to be easily understood and practicable. Being assisted by the leading cocking celebrities of this section, it is hoped and believed this treatise will be found adapted to all emergencies of the lovers of the beautiful and valiant bird known as the "Game Cock." Containing as it does the Standard Rules governing Cocking throughout the United States, Canada and Great Britain, carefully revised, together with a reliable course of treatment for all diseases incident to Game Fowls, this work should be in the hands of all interested in Cocking.

Our first edition having been received with such universal favor by both press and public, has caused the addition of several pages, illustrations and revisions, leaving nothing to be done to meet all requirements.

CONTENTS.

THE GAME COCK.

ORIGIN AND HISTORY OF THE GAME FOWL.

The Game Cock is vulgarly imagined to be the off-spring of the domesticated fowl and the pheasant. This idea is, however, not at all assented to by ornithologists, or the amateurs of the art of cocking. On more sure grounds its origin is referred to the wild cock of India, where he is occasionally seen in his wild state in the woods, and at the isles of St. Iago, Pulocondore, Timor, Phillippine and Mollucca islands, Sumatra, Java, New Guinea, Tinian, and the isles of the south seas. At Sumatra and Java they are noticed as being particularly large. Pliny, the historian, tells us that cock fighting was annually practiced at Pergamus, a city in Asia. The Athenians practised it at an annual festival, in the time of the great general, Themistocles, who encourged his soldiers to acts of bravery by admonishing them to imi-tate the example of the cock. Chalcis and Euboea were famous for their superior breed of cocks; they were large, and such as our sportsmen call shake bags or turn-outs. At Alexandria, in Egypt, they had a breed of hens which produced the best fighting cocks. The Romans were bet-ter acquainted with quails as fighting birds than with cocks. It is considered, however, that they were the first to introduce the practice in England, though the bird was there before Cæsar's arrival. Cocking was much en-couraged by Henry VIII, who founded the celebrated national cockpit at Westminster, afterwards renewed and encouraged by Charles II, who first introduced the breed of *pile* cocks, which for many years was held in such esti-mation, and by many much liked to this day.

In Cuba, Mexico, San Domingo and nearly all tropical

climates, cock fighting is one of the institutions of the
land. The Indian's idea of paradise, says a celebrated
author, is one vast cockpit; you never see the natives in
their full glory, but here the very Celestials are bitten
with the mania, and back their birds against anybody's.
The sport only takes place on Sundays and high days.
The betting is a perfect mania, but, to their praise be it
said, they are most honorable in paying what they have
lost. The cock's spurs are sharp as razors, and often one
or the other falls dead at first start. Should a cock show
any timidity, the niggers yell in the most frantic manner;
and, as there is always an unfortunate white feather
among the fowl, the above sound often fills the air on
Sunday afternoons. The match commences by two fel-
lows starting the cocks and getting their steam up. As
soon as No. 1 has beaten No. 2 there is a short rest, and
the next couple come on. This lasts till dusk, when "all
creation" may be seen coming out with dead and living
cocks; the village dominie is often a sportsman, and, after
instructing the interesting little natives in the way they
should go in the morning, in the afternoon he teaches the
cocks the way they should fight. On Sunday morning
he dons his clerical costume and exhorts his hearers, who
fill the church to overflowing. On Sunday afternoon he
exhorts his rooster and bets like any other mortal, sur-
rounded by his admiring assembly.

FORM AND PROPERTIES OF A FIGHTING COCK.

Having described the natural origin of this race of
birds and the history of the sport, we now proceed to
consider the general form and properties of the fighting
cock when in his greatest perfection, according to the
ideas now entertained. A good cock has eyes sparkling
with fire, boldness in his demeanor, and freedom in his
motions, and displays force in all his proportions. The
general outline of the finest cock, taken as a whole, ap-
proaches that of a lengthened cone or sugar loaf shape,
excluding the legs and tail, the apex of the cone being
the head and the base the vent and belly; under such external form may exist the best properties of the cock. In

describing the beauties of particular parts, the head
should be small, the beak strong and pointed, the neck
long and strong, the girth of the shoulders, chest and
body broad, feeling broad to the grasp, and tapering
again to the rump; the thighs and legs large and strong,
and rather long than short; with broad, thin feet, and
very long claws, a stately walk, and an upright, easy carriage, the wings not lying close on his back, but rather
extended. It is considered a good point if he brings his
legs close up to his body when held in the hand, instead
of letting them hang loosely down. It is a great property in a cock to be what is termed corky; that is, a cock
which, for its size, weighs light, having light flesh, and
light in the bone, though strong; they have a great advantage over lumpy cocks, which are heavy fleshed. A
sound cock will crow clear, having a clear, shining
feather, short, hard, and difficult to pluck from his body;
his face red, for if pale he is unhealthy. A good cock
should fight at any part of the body, and should carry a
fatal spur, or, in other words, hit well with his weapon.
Their actions should be quick, without hurrying, and
rapid, but cautious.

SOME OF THE DIFFERENT BREEDS OF FOWL.

The feathers afford a good criterion for judging of the
soundness of the bird; where they lie close to the skin
and compacted together, feel short and stiff to the touch,
and shining and glossy in their exterior, such is deemed a
sound feathered bird. The colors most admired are the
"reds" and the 'duck wings." By the red, among cockers, is understood a cock with a hackle (that is, the
feathers of the head and neck) red, with the feathers of
the rump and saddle to correspond. The red cock varies
with a black breast and ginger wing; that is, of a ginger-
bread color, or with a black breast and dark wing; such
are "dark reds." The "light reds" are those whose
breasts are wholly red, or red spotted with black, or black
streaked with red, and these receive their names according to these circumstances, as ginger breasted, spotted
breasted, etc. The "duck wing" cock derives his name
from a bar of steel blue across the greater coverts, like

the fascia across the wild duck's wing. In this case it is observed that the secondaries are exteriorly white; the hackle and saddle are also nearly the same color, or pale yellow, or cream colored; their breasts may be black, streaked or spotted; the shoulder may be tawny, dark red, or birchen, or silver shouldered, from which colors they receive their distinctions. The yellow cock is merely a variety of the "duck wing," from which it differs only in having the secondary feathers, or those next the flight, dark instead of white; the blue bar in these cocks sometimes varies to a light brown. The next color to be noticed is the "dun." These cocks are in reality of a lead, or slate color, and may be wholly so, or "duck wing," with the breast, flight and tail dun, or a yellow dun; that is, a yellow cock with a dun breast, flight and tail. By flight feathers are meant the strongest feathers of the wing farthest from the body of the cock when the wing is extended. The "red duns" are red cocks with dun breast, flight and tail. White cocks are either wholly white, and are called "smocks," or with red shoulders, and are called "piles;" when these are streaked with any other color in the hackle, breast, rump or tail, they are termed "streaky piles." If the pile cocks have a mixture of dun on the breast or shoulders, they are called "dun piles." Another variety of this breed is the "cuckoo," which is rare; he is white, with the feathers variegated promiscuously, or barred with black, yellow or red. The "spangle" is also rare; he is red, tipped with white spots, or white and black. "Hennies" have the natural propensities of the cock, but are so called from having the hackle, tail and wing more like the hen. When any colored fowl has the shoulder mixed with black he is called "beezy" shoulders, probably from the French word bis, black or dusky. The color of the legs should also be noticed; these are either yellow, black, white, blue, olive or dark green, willow or light green, or carp legged, which is a mixture of black and yellow. The beaks in general correspond with the color of the legs. The color of the eyes is also noticed in the match bill; the red or ferret eye (the iris being red), the pale yellow or daw eye, the dark brown or sloe eye.

Breeding for pit purposes and breeding for poultry shows are widely different, and in the latter respect only color and plumage count, as birds of the finest external appearance may, when they have to face the steels, turn out to be "bolters," whereas the less gaudily caparisoned cock, bred for the pit only, irrespective of color, generally fights to the death.

BREEDING.

A well tried breed of cocks, which have generally gained the odd battle when equally matched, being obtained, consider them the stock to breed from; the nearer their colors, the more kindly they will unite. Never breed from two old fowls; let one at least be young; be also thoroughly convinced that the cock is quite sound, by attending to his mode of feeding. Should he eat corn enough to make his crop very hard, and digest the same speedily, that is as sure a token his constitution is good, so that it is rotten when he eats but little, and has besides a bad digestion. To be still more sure, try also by running him down in a field, and sparring with another cock, at either of which, if he is unsound, he will turn black in the face. Try the hens in like manner. Three or four hens are enough for one cock. Let them be sisters if possible. The breeding place should be well aired, and entirely free from other fowl, lest the hens should be trod by other cocks. Clear water, grass, gravel, and lime rubbish, and an occasional change of food, is good—as barley, oats, potatoes, a little meat, toast and ale, etc. The roosts should be rather low, as the heavy fowls otherwise would, in descending, cripple themselves. The perches should be exactly suited to the grasp of the foot. The keeping of pigs, ducks, or allowing the fowl access to coal ashes or soap suds, produces the roop. There should be no geese or turkeys at the walk, as they are always battering the fowls. The nests should be made of clean, dry straw, rubbed soft between the hands, and put in a basket, earthen pan, or some such dish, and about a foot and a half from the ground. Hay is injurious to the eggs, faint in the smell, and is apt to engender vermin. There should be more nests than hens, as it will prevent them quarreling and breaking the eggs. One egg should always be marked with ink, and left in the nest for them to lay to, that you may know it from the others. As the eggs are laid, take them from the nest, mark and put them in bran, with the small end downwards. When a hen begins to cluck, do not save any more of her eggs for setting. If a cock dislikes any of the hens, she should be removed. About a dozen eggs are enough for a clutch. As the hen hatches the young, they may be taken and put in flannel, in a basket near the fire, till the last is hatched, feeding them three times a day till they rejoin their mother on crumbs of bread, hard boiled eggs, chopped raw meat, grits, etc.; and when returned to the mother, do it by night, when she is on the nest, otherwise she might fancy them strangers, and destroy them. They should then be conveyed to a dry place, where there are neither cats nor vermin, and for ten or twelve days the hen should be cooped, to prevent her from wandering and fatiguing the chickens; they should have clean water, fresh every day. At about six weeks old, when their sexes can be distinguished, select those which are to be kept, and destroy the rest, that the remaining ones may thrive the better by getting the whole attention of tho mother. Those chickens are of little value that are hatched later than May; and those hatched before the end of March are often cramped by cold; such as are later than the beginning of June never run cocks so high upon leg, light fleshed, or large boned. Cut the young cocks' combs at the age of four months, and about five or six weeks afterward their gills and deaf ears. The young cocks should be marked with scissors, by slitting part of the web of the foot, or cutting a small notch in the nostril, or punching a small hole in the web of the foot with a shoemaker's punch. Some do so to the web of the wing nearest the shoulder; others take a small notch out of the upper eyelid, by laying the scissors flat to the side of the head, and cutting out a very small piece of the lid. A clear air, good food and pure water, with perfect exclusion from other fowls, constitute the best walk, where, as before mentioned, they can obtain grass and gravel. At about a twelvemonth old they are called stags and two years old they are termed cocks. The short legged, or worst of your stags, should be tried against a good cock, to enable you to judge of the qualities of the remaining ones; for if he should beat the cock, there is every reason to consider the others good. Short spurs are best for this purpose.

It is always a sign of a hen being in good health, and clean fed, if the yolk of her egg, when boiled, is of a pale yellow; when of a dark red, the reverse. Chickens are

GAME COCK IN FEATHER.

composed of the tread and white of the egg, as the yolk comes to the world with them in their inside, on which they chiefly subsist, till they gain sufficient strength to follow their mother; for the first thing a hen gives her chickens is the small chips of broken shell out of which they come, which cut the yolk in their inside; and thereby promote digestion.

Fowls that once had the roop can never be entirely relied on as being either sound enough to breed from, or to fight.

TRAINING FOR THE PIT.

Suppose that the fowl comes from his walk in good condition, in which case he will be too fat for fighting, he must be reduced to give him wind. The general method of training is as follows:—First, cut his tail and spurs short and put him in the pens; no food the first day.

Second day, give him cream of tartar, or jalap or both united, about 6 or 8 grains, mixed with fresh butter and rock candy. Immediately after he gets the physic, tie on the bots, or muffles, and spar him with another cock on a straw or grass plat, till he gets fatigued; then return him to his pen; but if his mouth has been pecked, rub it with a little vinegar and good brandy mixed, to prevent it from cankering. Then give him a warm mess, to work off his physic, which you must make of bread and milk and a little rock candy, or ale and bread and rock candy, giving him a large tea cup full; when he gets this, shut him up till next morning. If cold weather, cover him up with a blanket, or keep fire in the room; if warm, clip him out; also keep him dark, by shutting the windows always, except at feeding times. Weigh them the third day when empty, and the moment they are weighed let them begin to feed.

Third day, clean out his pen from the effects of the physic, giving clean, dry straw; also, wash his legs, feet and face, before putting him among this clean straw. He is next to be allowed some cock bread, made of the following ingredients:—About three pounds of fine flour and two eggs, and four whites of eggs, and a little yeast, kneaded with a proper quantity of water, and have it well baked in an oven; to which you may add a small number of aniseeds or a little cinnamon; cut this in small pieces, give one cup full in the morning, and one in the evening, allowing no water the third day with the above bread.

Fourth morning, he should have half a teacup full of good barley and a little water, in which a piece of toast has been steeped; having eaten this, clean his pen and give new straw, leaving his pen uncovered about an hour, to allow him to scratch himself. The barley should be hard chaffed, to take away the sharp points; in the afternoon, the same quantity of barley, but no water.

Fifth day, bread as before, in three quantities, but no water.

Sixth day, bread early in the morning, and towards the afternoon a good feed of barley and water. Some feeders give sheep's heart, cut small, both this and the succeeding day, mixed with the other food.

Seventh day, a feed of barley early in the morning; in the afternoon, bread and the white of an egg boiled hard, allowing him also a little water.

Eighth day, or day of fighting, allow him about 40 grains of barley, and one or two mouthsfull of water from a toast, apple or cheese, for digesting; hemp seed, steeped in brandy, prevents purging. Wheat or millet seed may be added to his food, sometimes hemp seed as a small mixture. Bread toast, soaked in vinegar, is sometimes given for reducing quickly.

The following is another method of preparing cocks for battle:—After cautiously examining whether the cocks are sound and hard-feathered, keep them in separate pens, with moveable perches within; keep the pens peculiarly clean, and feed them with the crumb of stale bread cut into square pieces, giving each a handful at sunrise, noon and sunset, with cool spring water for drink; after thus feeding for four or five days, let them spar some morning with one another in a room covered with straw, or on a grass plot, first guarding their heels with mufflers; let them spar some time, but not so far as to draw blood. When they pant and appear faint, give to each about the size of a walnut of white rock candy, rosemary chopped, and butter, mixed together; this will increase their strength, cleanse them, and render them long-winded; immediately after this, put them into separate bags or baskets half filled with straw, then cover them with the

same material, and make them fast, in order that the
cocks may sweat till evening; at night take them out, lick
their eyes and head all over with the tongue, fill their
throats with stale bread, and pour warm urine therein,
which will cleanse both their heads and bodies. Exercise
by commencing with 25 flies, and increase daily till you
have reached about 300, and diet them with stale bread
and whites of eggs regularly, one day sparring or flying,
and the other feeding and resting, with now and then
the scouring, for about a fortnight previous to the battle.

The muffles or gloves should be made of chamois
leather, about the size of a small egg, stuffed with wad-
ding, wool or curled hair, with a string at the opening, to
draw it together. Put this bag over the natural heel,
draw it together and tie around the leg. Then spar your
fowl with these on them. When you wish to test the
gameness of a fowl place a cork over the steel spur, leaving the point exposed, so that it will prick the bird sufficient to try gameness, but not so as to inflict severe injury.

MODE OF TRIMMING.

After having tied your fowl's legs with a handkerchief
or a piece of soft string, place him on your lap, with his
legs between your knees, and his head toward yourself;
then, collecting all his neck feathers together, apply your
forefinger and thumb in a circular form to that part of
the neck next the shoulder of the cock, and press forward
the whole of his neck feathers as close round his head as
possible; they will then appear like an erect frill round his
head; to which apply a long and sharp pair of scissors as
close to your finger and thumb as possible all round, and
then take off the surface of the remaining ones next the
head, but not too bare; in fact, it is performed on the
same principle as hair cutting; for the feathers are short-
ened by being cut when turned the contrary way to that
in which they naturally lie. Next cut about two inches
off the ends of both his wings, at the same time making
the flight feathers decrease in length a quarter of an inch
in proportion to the others, leaving the flight feathers
farthest from his body the shortest, which should be at

least three inches from its insertion in the wing. Then
cut the tail, leaving it a large hand's breadth from its insertion in the rump outwards, taking off all the curling
feathers round it, leaving only the vane or fan. When his
tail is perfectly erect apply the scissors (with their point
inclining a little downward) to the saddle, cutting from a
line with the lower feathers of the tail toward the end
of the wing; some in trimming cut out a great quantity
of the soft feathers from under the saddle, to keep the
cocks cool. All the feathers round the vent are cut off
very close from under the tail to three or four inches toward the breast between the legs. His spurs are cut off
with a thin saw, leaving about a quarter of an inch on
the leg, on which is fixed the steel spur; sometimes, when
the spur is so sawed off, blood will issue from it, which
may be stopped immediately by rubbing a piece of chalk
firmly into it, or applying a hot iron.

DIRECTIONS FOR HEELING.

In tieing on the spur, take a piece of soft, thin brown
paper, and, having folded it two or three times, and having dampened it a little with the tongue, wrap it around
the remaining quarter of an inch of his natural heel as
often as you think there will be room in the socket of the
steel spur to contain it and the natural spur together;
then place the steel spur on the natural spur, pressing
the socket close to the leg, observing at the same time
that the curved part of the spur is next the foot, and the
hollow side upwards, or, in other words, the point inclining upwards; it should stand much in the same direc-
tion with the natural spur; or, if you take a view from
the point to the socket, the point should then appear on
a line with the hollow of the inside of the leg; then lap
the leather ends over each other, and tie them down with
a piece of waxed string about the thickness of a shoemaker's thread, beginning with the middle of the thread
on the socket of the spur, close to the spur, going round
the leather close to the socket on both sides with the
string as often as is necessary for security; this should
neither be too tight to cramp him, nor so loose as to

come off; for should it come off during the battle, or break, it is not allowed to be replaced. A fair spur should be round and smooth from the socket to the point; if flat on any side, or rough, it is foul and improper.

The subjoined is another method of heeling:—Let your fowl be held by a competent person; let him be held so that the inside of the leg is perfectly level, then take your thumb and forefinger and work the back toe of the fowl. While doing this you will see the leader of the leg rise and fall at the upper joint. You will set the right spur on a line with the outside of the leader, at the upper joint of the leg; and the left spur you will set on a line with the inside of the leader, at the upper joint. Be careful not to set the spur too far in, as it would cause the cock to cut himself. As a general rule for a young beginner, he had better set the right spur on a line with the outside of the leg, opposite to the upper joint; and the left spur on a line with the outside of the leader of the upper joint. Cover the spur with a piece of damp paper, or very soft buckskin, so as to get the socket of the spur to fit tightly, and to prevent its turning or shifting. When you have the spur arranged properly, tie it with good wax ends, but not so tight as to cramp the legs or toes of the fowls.

ABOUT MAINS.

There are three kinds of mains, or matches, at present in use among cockers. The long main, which generally continues for a week; the short main of a day or two (both regulated by the same laws), and the Welsh main. In the long main the cocks are generally the property of a joint subscription, or of only two individuals, and the cocks thus collected are chosen for the main according to their weights, those being preferred, as a medium weight, from three pounds eight ounces to four pounds ten ounces, giving or taking an ounce on either side, though they are generally matched to a drachm weight. The cocks which form the bye battles of the main become the objects of separate betting, and are subject to the same regulations. Cocks which weigh above four pounds ten ounces are termed turn out, and are never matched by weight, as when they weigh above that they are reckoned fit to contend with any one.

The short main lasts only for a day or two, the cocks being fewer in number, or the numbers are doubled for each day.

The Welsh main is generally fought for a purse, or prize. In this main all the fowls are restricted to a certain weight, viz., about four pounds four ounces; these are matched according as shall be agreed upon, the winners again taking the winners till they are reduced to the last pair, when the winner of the last battle gains the prize. Besides this, there is to be noticed the battle royal, which consists of a number of fowls being put down together at the same time in the pit, and the last survivor gains the prize—a practice known nowhere but in England.

In fighting a regular main they always commence with the lightest cocks, as they can be first prepared, and the heaviest ones, that have been most reduced by this means, gain time to recover their strength and be brought up again.

FORM OF ARTICLES.

Articles of agreement, made the ————— day of ————— one thousand eight hundred and —————, between —————. First, the said parties have agreed that each of them shall produce, show and weigh, at —————, on the ————— day of————— —————, beginning at the hour of —————, cocks not under —————, nor above —————, and as many of each party's cocks that come within one ounce of each other shall fight for ————— a battle; that is, ————— each cock, in as equal divisions as the battles can be divided into six pits, or day's play, at the cock-pit before mentioned, and the party's cocks that win the greatest number of battles, matched out of the number before specified, shall be entitled to the sum of —————, odd battle money, and the sum to be staked in the hands of Mr. —————, before any cocks are pitted, by both parties; and we further agree to produce, show and weigh, on the said weighing days, ————— cocks for ————— bye battles, subject to the same weight as the cocks in the main, and these to be added to the number of cocks unmatched; and as many of them as come within one ounce of each other shall fight for ————— a battle; the number of cocks so matched to be equally divided as will permit of, and added to each day's play with the main cocks; and it is also agreed that the balance of the battle money shall be paid at the end of each day's play ; it is also further agreed that the cocks fight with steel spurs, and with fair hackles, and to be subject to all the usual rules of cock fighting, and the profits arising from the spectators, called door money, to be equally divided between both parties, after all charges are paid that usually happen on these occasions. Witness our hands this ———— day of ———— 18—.

ENGLISH GENERAL LAWS OF COCKING

It is understood on all occasions that when the cocks are once pitted, the setters-to are not allowed to handle them; unless they get entangled in each other, or in the mat, it is fair to turn them on their feet again. On no pretence are feathers to be removed from the beak or eyes during the fight. If one of the cocks is hit down during the battle, and no longer able to fight, take the first opportunity (while the other is not fighting him) of telling the "short law," which you do by counting, distinctly and audibly, "twice twenty," when they may be handled and set-to again. If the weakest then refuses, you begin to tell the "long law" of one hundred, by counting it by tens. At the end of each time you count ten, set them to, beak to beak, and if either cock refuses to fight ten times successively, he loses; but should he show fight, by pecking or fighting at the other, while you are counting the one hundred, you must begin with your tens again, and at the end of each ten you must say aloud, "once refused," "twice refused," &c., till he refuses ten times, when you may withdraw your cock and claim the battle money. Should both be disabled and refuse to fight before the "long law" begins counting, it is a drawn battle, and neither wins; and should both refuse fighting during the telling of the "long law," it is that cock's battle which fought last. If any one wishes to stop this telling him out, he may "pound him." In this case he lays down his hat or anything else on the pit, as a token of the challenge, when the "short law" is told by a person distinctly counting twice twenty, and afterwards repeating the words, "will any one take it?" three times; if no one accepts the challenge during this "short law," the cock is beaten. It is necessary, when any one takes the poundage or bet, that he declares it, and also lays down something on the pit as surety. If so, the cock must fight till death, though sometimes he unexpectedly recovers and wins.

On the day of weighing, he whose chance it is to weigh last is to set his cocks and number his pens, both byes and main, and deposit the key of the pens upon the weighing table (or the adversary may put a lock upon the door) before any cock is put into the scales; and after the first pack of cocks is weighed, a person appointed by him that weighed first shall go into the other pens to see that no other cocks are weighed but what are numbered and so set, if they are within the articles of weight that the match specifies; but if not, to take the following cock or cocks, until all the number of main and bye cocks are weighed through. When they are all weighed, proceed directly to match them, with the least weight first, and so on; and equal weights or nearest weights to be separated, if by that separation an increased number of battles can be made; all blanks must be filled up on the weighing day, and the battles struck off and divided for each day's play, as previously agreed on, and the cocks that weigh the least are to fight the first day, and so upward.

At the time assented to by both parties, the cocks that are to fight the first battle are produced upon the pit by the feeders or their helpers; and after an examination to see whether they correspond with the marks and colors stated in the match bill, they are given to the setters-to, who, after chopping them in hand, give them to the masters of the match (who always sit fronting each other), when they turn them down upon the mat; and by no means are the setters-to to touch them, except they should hang in the mat, in each other, or get close to the pit's edge, until they shall cease fighting, while a person can tell forty. When both cocks leave off fighting until one of the setters-to, or one appointed for stating the law, can tell forty gradually, then the setters-to are to make the nearest way to their cocks, and when they have taken them up, to carry them into the middle of the pit, and directly deliver them on their legs, beak to beak, and not to touch them again until they have refused fighting, so long as the teller of the law can tell ten, unless they are on their backs, or hung in each other, or in the mat; then again they are to set-to as before, and continue it till one cock refuses fighting ten several times, one after another, when it is that cock's victory that fought within the law. Now and then it happens that both cocks refuse fighting while the law is telling; in this case a fresh cock is to be hoveled, and brought forward upon the mat as soon as possible, and the setters-to are to toss up which cock is to be set-to first, and he that gets the chance has the choice. Then the other which is to be set-to last must be taken up, but not carried off the pit, and setting the hoveled cock down to the other five separate times, telling ten between each setting-to, and the same to the other cock; if one fights, and the other declines, the fighting cock has the battle; should both fight, or both refuse, it is a drawn battle. The meaning of setting-to five times to each cock is, that ten times setting-to being the long law, so, on their both refusing, the law is to be equally shared between them.

Deciding a battle by another way is, if any one offers to lay ten to one, and no one takes it until the law teller counts forty, and calls out three separate times:— "Will any one take it?" and if no one does, it is that cock's battle the odds are laid on, and the setters-to are not to touch the cocks all the time the forty is telling, unless either cock is hung in the mat, or on his back, or hung together. If a cock should die before the "long law" is told out, notwithstanding he fought in the law, and the other did not, he loses the battle.

There are often disputes in setting-to in the "long law," for frequently both cocks refuse fighting until four or five, or more or less times are told; then they sometimes commence telling from that cock's fighting, and counting but once refused, but they should continue their counting on, until one cock has refused ten times; for it is for both cocks when the law is begun to be told; and if one cock fights within the "long law," and the other not, it is a battle to the cock that fought, reckoning from the first setting-to. All disputes relative to bets, or the battle being gained or lost, must be decided by the spectators. The crowing and mantling of a cock, or fighting at the setter-to's hands before he is put to the other cock, or breaking from his adversary, is not allowed as a fight.

COCKERS' TRICKS EXPOSED.

1. The person who seconds, or sets-to the cock, may break his thigh with his fingers and thumb in a moment,

or may (by pressing his thumbs hard on his kidneys, or by griping him severely by the vent) cause him to lose the battle, though otherwise he could have won it; this will depend on his regard for his employer, or the understanding between him and the opposite party; for if he thinks he can get more from them as a bribe to sell the fight than he expects from the person who employs him, he will act the above dishonorable part, and for this reason it is advisable for every person to second his own fowl, except there is a very good understanding indeed between him and the person he employs for that purpose.

2. If the employer or his second allow the cock to go into the hands of any other person previous to the battle, he may be crippled in an instant, as the person so handling him might have an interest in seeing him beaten.

3. If one cock sticks with his spurs into the other, the second of the cock who has received the blow takes out the spur, for if this be entrusted to the other second, he has it in his power to wrench the spur in different directions in taking it out, and do the fowl a serious injury, and might (with the point) rip a hole in him that would bleed him to death; this must be guarded against.

4. Very often the opposite second pretends not to know that his cock has stuck in the other; he immediately catches him up as high as he can reach, and nearly drags the head from the body of the other, or allows him to fall with great force on the pit.

5. If a cock has but one eye he should not be pitted till the second is convinced that he sees his antagonist, but if the opposite second can, he will pit his one on the blind side; beware of that.

6. Some have a trick of using foul spurs. These appear round on one side, but on the upper side, or that next the body of the cock, they are sharpened with an edge like a knife; others are three edged, or bayonet pointed, which are also foul; in fact, one cannot be too particular in examining the opponent's spurs, which, to be fair, should be perfectly round to the socket, and smooth or polished.

7. When both cocks are so distressed that neither can scarcely hold up his head, and perhaps the one can no longer peck his antagonist, the second of this last mentioned one, in setting him to with the other, beak to beak, raises his head with one hand, and, with the other, by suddenly raising his tail, bobs him on the other cock, and makes it appear as if he had chopped or pecked, when no such thing took place; this must be strictly watched

8. If a cock, after having chopped, becomes so weak as to be unable to do so again, his second, in pretending to set him to, beak to beak, with the other, only puts him near him, and allows his head to drop under the breast of the other, to prevent him from feeling him, who might chop in return and win the battle; they should always in the "long law" be put fairly beak to beak.

9. If the opponent's cock is a good mouthed cock in distress—that is, one who will readily take hold and fight— his second will place his beak on the neck or shoulder of the other, which gives him a great advantage, if permitted, but is unfair and not admissible.

10. The same person will sometimes have two cocks taken to the pit, one carried by himself and the other by his friend or some other person, who pretend to know nothing of each other. They then (to appearance) make up a match between the said two cocks, all the while well knowing which is to win, as the one is previously known to be bad and the other good; this is another system in betting, by which they deceive and rob the spectators, for they are then safe in betting any odds, and the long odds are generally taken. There are various tricks practised by such parties, but keen observation and second thoughts will avert them.

11. A person will show a cock with particular marks and color, in full feather, which he matches against another equal in weight; he then retires to trim him for the fight, but returns with another, marked and colored like the first, but much larger, gaining by this manœuvre a decided advantage; this is called "Ringing the changes."

12. Sometimes they will rub the face of a sound, healthy cock, with flour and grease, or chalk and grease, to make

him look stale, or with grease and blacking, to make him look rotten; at the same time he may be as good as any between "earth and sky."

13. If the opposite party wish to gain an advantage in weight, they will first see your bird weighed; then one of them may take a two or four ounce weight, the hollow of which is filled with tallow grease, and stick it close to the bottom of the scale in which the proper weights are, unseen, if possible; and by these means make their cock, which is two or four ounces heavier than the other, appear the same weight. The scales, therefore, should be narrowly examined, and even if you do not look up at the beam the slightest touch of a small stick, or the brim of a hat on some one's head, will make all the difference.

14. The fowl or fowls of both parties should be weighed by the very same weights; for, if the least chance is afforded, false ones may be substituted.

15. Cocks that are intended for battle should never be seen or touched by any one but the master or the feeder, otherwise you are never safe; for they might mix your cock's food with the victuals taken out of the crop of another almost dead with the roop.

Cocks that are meant to fight by gas light should receive the last meals by gas or candle light each day, about the hour appointed for the contest.

16. Take great care who you allow to tie on the spurs, as they might be too tight, and cramp the cock, or loose, and come off.

A FEW HINTS ON SPURS.

One of the most important matters to be attended to is the gaffs, or spurs, as on these depend the issue of most contests. In the olden times the cock spur was made of silver, but for the past half century those made of steel have had the preference. There is a large variety of spurs in use, nearly every section of country varying more or less in size and style. The regulation spur governing

PATTERNS OF SPURS.

Regulation One and a Quarter Inch Spur.

Drop Socket Two Inch Spur.

Front Drop Socket Two Inch Spur.

New York state measures one and a quarter inch from
the top rim of the socket to the extreme point of the
blade, which is round, tapering to a fine point, and di-
verging from the socket outwards in a slight curve upwards. The spurs should be of the very best tempered
steel, must be finely finished, and of such a quality as to
stand being struck into hard wood without fear of breaking. Very few understand properly the manufacturing
of gaffs, and those sold by large importing houses of re-
puted standing and integrity are, as a general thing,
worthless, the material of which they are composed being
little better than lead, and the sockets not half large
enough to go over the natural heel. The style of gaff
known as the drop socket is so called from the blade
dropping downwards at the socket, and although considered unfair is much in use all over this country. They
are much more severe in execution and make shorter
work of the sport. There are also sword-blades, dia-
mond blades, slashers and a variety of other spurs, some
of them being from four to five inches in length. All of
these are unfair, however, except in those parts where
they are tolerated.

For turn-outs, no longer than two inches and a half
spurs should be used; for lesser ones, from two inches to
two and a quarter; for cocks of four pounds four ounces,
not more than two inches; and if under four pounds, one
inch and a half, or shorter; for when they come to grap-
pling in close quarters or in distress, a long spur is almost
useless; it may do for a dash or two at the first onset,
but not afterwards.

ORIGIN OF DISEASES.

Club foot is an ailing which generally shows itself in large fowls, and arises from flying off high places and causing too severe a jar.

Rheumatism is noticed in fowls in mid-summer, after much damp and rainy weather, and sometimes comes from plunging them in water for the hatching fever.

Pip is confined to young fowls during the hotter months, and is attributed to unclean food, dirty water, cold, damp localities, or from drinking rain water.

Inflammation of the eye originates from exposure to cold and moist weather, attended with easterly winds.

Costiveness arises from dry diet, without access to vegetables—the latter they should always be furnished with. The chickens should be furnished with chick weed, tender grass, green cabbage, etc.

Asthma is caused by obstruction of the air cells and an accumulation of phlegm, which interferes with the exercise of their function and causes them to labor for breath.

Chicken pox is generally the result of fighting, when the head has been badly pecked. It will come sometimes without any apparent cause, and will affect a number at the same time.

Cholera is a disease of recent introduction, and in some instances the fowl dies in less than an hour after it is attacked. Upon dissection the liver is found much enlarged, and a sticky, slimy substance covers the surface. This slime everywhere appears to pervade the mucus membrane, and clogging up the air passages, produces death.

Moulting, or shedding the feathers, is of annual occurrence, and frequently requires treatment; after the third year, fowls moult later every succeeding year, and it is often as late as January before old fowls come into feather. The time of moulting continues according to age, health and weather, from six weeks to three months.

Megrims is brought on from overfeeding, want of exercise, and from having no shelter from the powerful sun, which effects the birds' heads, and they become stupid and giddy.

Paralysis arises from various causes, but principally from fowls being confined in small, damp and unhealthy yards.

Appoplexy arises from overfeeding; want of exercise and foul water frequently bring on fits of appoplexy, and numbers of fowls drop from their roosts and die in a few seconds.

Snuffles is brought on by cold, continued feeding on dry husky corn, confinement and requirement of green food. The birds' throats become sore and, unless some soft, nourishing food is given them immediately, they lose flesh rapidly.

Yellows arises from the fowls having been fed on sour, unwholesome corn.

Crop-bound arises from the birds having been kept short of food for several days and then over fed with a quantity of dry corn, they consequently over-gorge themselves, and, from weakness, cannot digest the food.

Cramp is generally caused by cold, damp and unhealthy places in which fowls are often kept, and it effects them principally in the legs.

DISEASES AND THEIR CURE.

ROUP

Symptoms.—Rising and falling of the wattle in breathing, whooping sound in the throat, offensive discharge from the nostrils, occasionally the head and eyes become swollen and feverish, which, if not attended to, will form matter in the eyes; this requires prompt attention or it will destroy the sight.

Treatment.—Separate the fowl affected as above and put in a warm box with straw, changing the straw daily. Bathe head and throat with warm salted water, after which open the eyes and wash, with the end of a rag, saturated in the water. Give a pill composed of chalk and cayenne pepper, mixed equally, every morning. If a rattling in the throat, give one teaspoonful of cod liver oil every night. After three or four days, if improved, tie the fowl by the leg and let it out in the sunshine, returning it to its warm box every night.

CHOLERA.

Symptoms.—A drooping of the wings, and a sticky slime in the mouth and throat.

Treatment.—Give to the fowl affected with cholera one pill every day, the size of a common marble, prepared of cayenne pepper two parts, prepared chalk two parts, pulverized gentian one part, pulverized charcoal one part; mix all well together into a paste with lard. Keep the fowl dry and warm for forty-eight hours. Do not give water. As a preventive, make a paste of cayenne pepper one part, prepared chalk one part, pulverized gentian two parts, and pulverized charcoal two parts, mixed with lard.

In case the disease is in your neighborhood, give an ordinary sized pill once a week to the grown fowls.

PIP OR GAPES.

Symptoms.—Gapes are formed from worms in the windpipe; the membrane of the tongue is thickened, particularly towards the windpipe, breathing is impeded, and the bill often held open, as if gasping for breath.

Treatment.—Cut off the tip end of the tongue, give a small pill once a day, composed of prepared chalk and ground black pepper of equal proportions, and made into a paste with lard. When mixed, add a few drops of oil of wormseed, and mix it well with the paste. Pills of all kinds must be forced down the throat.

RHEUMATISM, OR LIFTS.

Symptoms.—Stiffness of the limbs and joints, lifting the feet high, slow, and as if in pain, while others jerk by starts.

Treatment.—Bathe the upper joint of the thigh with spirits or alcohol, dry it in well, then make an ointment of fish-worms, simmer them down in butter, then strain and grease the whole leg and thigh every day. Do not be content with a few trials of this remedy, but give it a fair chance.

GOUT.

This disease is generally confined to old fowls, and is known by swelling of the joints; it should be treated the same as rheumatism.

CLUB FOOT.

Treatment.—Scarify the limb with a sharp knife or a scalpel, cut just through the skin, begin on the outside of the lump and let all the cuts run to the centre. Then scrape out all the coagulated blood that the tumor contains, and well cleaned, bring all the flaps to the centre; then double a strip of muslin four or five times; have it large enough to cover all the sole of the foot; place this over the flaps when brought together, then tie with narrow strips of muslin or broad tape; bring it through the toes so as to have it well tied, or sewed fast above, which is better. Secure it so that it cannot come off; let it remain so for one or two weeks, then take it off and you will find the foot nearly well.

INFLAMMATION OF THE EYE.

Symptoms.—Small abscesses are formed on the cornea, which are filled with a white colored pus. The eye becomes inflamed, the lids swelling to a great extent, and a coagulable matter, like the white of an egg, accumulates beneath the swelling.

Treatment.—Bathe the head and throat with hot salted water, then remove any pus that has accumulated in the eye, after which wash the eye out by holding the lids open and fill the eye up with fine table salt. Pour down the fowl's throat half teaspoonful of fine, dry, black pepper. Repeat this treatmeat once a day, keeping the fowl in a warm, dry place, and place him in the sun for a few hours every day.

INDIGESTION.

Treatment.—Exercise the fowl daily, give him less food and a large pill, made of Cayenne pepper one part, prepared chalk one part, pulverized gentian two parts, pulverized charcoal two parts, mixed into a paste with lard. Feed with a baked cake composed of corn meal, crumbs of bread and egg soaked in good ale.

COSTIVENESS.

Treatment.—Give as much pulverized rhubarb as will lay on a two cent piece, to open the bowels.

DIARRHŒA.

Symptoms.—Diarrhœa resembles the yolk of a stale egg sticking to the feathers near the vent.

Treatment.—Physic with pulverized rhubarb as much as will lay on a silver quarter. Then give daily for several days the following pill:—Prepared chalk three parts, cayenne pepper one part, pulverized gentian one part, pulverized charcoal one part, mixed with lard or butter. The pill should be the size of a common marble. Keep the fowl in a warm place for a few days, after which let him run at large in the sunshine.

OBSTRUCTIONS OF THE NOSTRIL.

Symptoms.—When produced by fighting it forms a hard crust, and the fowl gasps for breath.

Treatment.—Wash the head with wine, afterwards grease with sweet oil.

CANKER.

Symptoms.—The mouth and inside of the bill has a very fetid smell; the canker substance is yellow.

Treatment.—Scrape off all the yellow substance with a small stick, and if the fowl bleeds it will do no injury. Then rub with the thumb or forefinger the diseased parts with fine, dry table salt. Also, give the fowl half a teaspoonful of dry cayenne pepper inwardly. Repeat this process daily.

ASTHMA.

Treatment.—Physic with pulverized rhubarb, bathe the head with warm salt water, give a teaspoonful of vinegar every morning, and half a teaspoonful of fine black pepper at night.

MELANCHOLY.

Symptoms.—Want of appetite, drooping, etc.

Treatment.—Physic with pulverized rhubarb, then give a cholera pill daily composed of cayenne pepper two parts, prepared chalk two parts, pulverized gentian one part, pulverized charcoal one part, mixed into a paste with lard, and occasionally half a teaspoonful of vinegar inwardly. For diet, give meal mixed with a little fennel seed, dragon's blood, and wet it with good draft ale.

FEVER.

Symptoms.—Redness of the eye, hot head, drooping, etc.

Treatment.—Give a little nitre in water, and physic with pulverized rhubarb.

CONSUMPTION.

Symptoms.—Hoarseness, sneezing, etc.

Treatment.—They should be sheltered and well housed, and sometimes wrapped up in warm flannel; keep them near the fire until they liven up.

LIMED LEGS.

Symptoms.—The legs of the fowl have the appearance of their having been walking through wet lime, the whitish appearance increasing until the scales of the leg will raise up like large warts; the leg enlarges and gets rough to the touch, extending above the leg, in which locality the skin looks inflamed and flabby, and the flesh falls away.

Treatment.—Grease the parts affected thoroughly, every second or third day, with sweet oil and spirits of turpentine (equal parts), well shaken before being used.

CHICKEN POX

Symptoms.—Small specks scattered over the head and throat, which enlarge and spread all over the head and close the eyes.

Treatment.—Physic with pulverized rhubarb, and grease the parts affected once a day with equal parts of sweet oil and spirits of turpentine, regardless of the eyes, as it will not hurt them. When scabs form, each day before applying the mixture, take a stick and scrape all the scabs off. Don't mind bleeding. After scraping off clean, grease the head and throat all over. Stuff the fowl once a day with warm milk and bread, and plenty of pepper.

MOULTING.

Symptoms.—Loss of appetite, inactivity, moping and loss of feathers.

Treatment.—Keep warm, feed well, and mix pulverized ginger with their food; give plenty of meat, and change frequently to induce appetite.

LOSS OF FEATHERS.

Symptoms.—The same as in Moulting, except that the lost feathers are not supplied by new ones, and the bare skin is quite rough.

Treatment.—Grease the parts affected with lard mixed in sulphur and gunpowder, also apply sweet oil and turpentine, equal parts, shake up before using. For diet, mix a little flour of sulphur and cayenne pepper with their food. A good walk, grass and fresh water are indispensable.

MEGRIMS.

Treatment.—Bathe their heads with cold water, and give a dose of castor oil every other morning during the week. Feed on boiled rice, potatoes, and thin oat-meal.

APPOPLEXY.

Treatment.—Feed light, without corn for a week; give a dessert spoonful of castor oil three times a week.

SNUFFLES.

Treatment.—Give bread, scalded milk, with a lump of lard in it, warm, for their food.

PARALYSIS.

Treatment.—Give a dessert spoonful of castor oil, keep warm, change food and ground. Change of air often restores the bird to a healthy state. The corn must be old and good, and fresh water should be placed in the fountains every morning.

YELLOWS.

Symptoms.—The skin of the bird turns dark yellow.
Treatment.—Give the fowl barley-meal and oat-meal mixed with brown sugar and milk, also 1 oz. of tincture of bark with 3 ozs. of water may be given during the week.

CROP-BOUND.

Treatment.—Give a dose of castor oil, 1 oz., and should this fail, open the crop with a sharp penknife and remove the hardened mass. The crop can be easily sown, and there is not the slightest danger in this operation, if it be skilfully performed.

CRAMP.

Treatment.—Place the fowl's legs in hot water for twenty minutes, then rub dry and put him in a warm place, feed on barley-meal, hempseed and maize, with plenty of green food and clean water.

COCK FIGHTING RULES.

SYRACUSE (N. Y.,) RULES.

1. The pit shall be at least twelve feet square, with a board two feet six inches long across each corner, and eighteen inches high, the bottom covered with sawdust, tanbark or carpet, as shall be agreed upon; there shall be a line drawn across the centre, and one a foot each way from the centre line.

2. Each pitter shall choose an umpire, the umpires to choose a referee whose decision, when the umpires cannot agree, shall be final.

3. After the first handling the cocks shall be delivered on the outer lines square on their feet.

4. A fair inch and a quarter round heel to be used, unless otherwise agreed upon.

5. Chickens shall take their age from the first day of March, and shall be chickens during the following fighting season; that is, for the following fifteen months.

6. The hackle to be cut off or not, as the parties shall agree upon.

7. The pitter shall not handle his cock after being delivered in the pit without counting ten and his adversary's cock refusing to fight, except that he is fast in the pit, in himself, or in the other cock.

8. A cock on his back can be turned on his side, or if his wing is out it can be placed under him without putting him on his feet.

9. No pitter shall draw his own heel when he is fast in the other cock.

10. In billing the cocks before the fight, if one cock refuses and the other shows fight, the one showing shall win the match.

11. The pitter who has the count shall count ten five times, naming each ten as once, twice, and so on, and shall handle after each ten, and after the fifth ten the cocks shall be fairly breasted; he is then to count thirty and breast them twenty and out.

12. When a cock is pounded, and no one takes it, the pitter of the cock the odds are on shall count twenty, say, "Who takes it?" three times, and win. If the poundage is taken, the pitter shall count as if there was no poundage; the poundage shall be twenty dollars to

one, to be thrown into the pit or put up in the referee's hands, the pitter to be satisfied that the money is up; if this is not done the pitter is to count as if there was no poundage.

13. The pitter of the cock making fight last to have the count.

14. If a cock is pounded and the poundage is taken, then if the cock the odds are against shall knock down the other cock, and the other cock is pounded, if the pitter of the cock pounded last shall count twenty, say "Who takes?" three times before the poundage is taken, he shall win the fight.

15. After the cock has been delivered, the pitter shall not clean his cock's beak or eyes, nor squeeze or press him against the ground.

16. The cock having the count wins the fight if he dies before the count is out. A cock breaking to get away is not a fighting cock.

17. Neither cock to be taken from the pit or the heels taken off without the referee's consent.

18. A man fighting a cock heavier than represented in the marked list shall lose the fight, although he wins. The cocks to be weighed before leaving the pit; if both cocks are over weight the fight is a draw.

19. In case of appeal, the fighting shall cease until the decision is given.

20. All bets to follow the referee's decision.

21. Any violation of the above rules loses the match.

NEW YORK RULES.

ARTICLE 1. The pit shall be a circular pit, at least eighteen feet in diameter and not less than sixteen inches in height, the floor of which shall be covered with carpet or some other suitable material. There shall be a chalk or other mark made as near as can be to the centre of the pit. There shall also be two outer marks, which shall be one foot each way from the centre mark.

2. The pitters shall each choose one judge, who shall choose a referee. Said judge shall decide all matters in dispute during the pendency of the fight, but, in case of their inability to agree, then it shall be the duty of the referee to decide, and his decision shall be final.

3. Chickens shall take their age from the 1st day of March, and shall be chickens during the following fighting season, to wit:— From the 1st day of March, 1873, to the 1st day of June, 1874.

4. It shall be deemed foul for either of the respective pitters to pit a cock or chicken with what is termed a foul hackle—that is, any of the feathers left whole on the mane or neck.

5. The pitters shall let each cock bill each other three or more times, but this is not to be so construed that the pitter of a cock has a right to bill with his opponent's cock for the purpose of fatiguing him.

6. No person shall be permitted to handle his fowl after he is fairly delivered in the pit, unless he counts ten, clear and distinct, without either cock making fight; or shall be fast in his adversary, or fast in the carpet, or hung in the web of the pit, or in himself.

7. Any cock that may get on his back, the pitter thereof shall turn him off it, but not take him off the ground he is lying on.

8. Whenever a cock is fast in his adversary, the pitter of the cock the spurs are fast in shall draw them out, but the pitter of a cock has no right to draw out his own spur, except when fast in himself, or in the carpet, or in the web of the pit.

9. When either pitter shall have counted ten tens successively, without the cock refusing fight, making fight, again breasting them fair on their feet, breast to breast and beak to beak, on the centre score or mark, on the fifth ten being told, and also on the ninth ten being told, shall have won the fight. The pitters are bound to tell each ten as they count them, as follows:—Once, twice, etc.

10. No pitter, after the cocks have been delivered in the pit, shall be permitted to clean their beaks, or eyes, by blowing or otherwise, or of squeezing his fowl, or pressing him against the floor during the pendency of a fight.

11. When a cock is pounded, and no person takes it until the pitter counts twenty twice, and calls three times "Who takes it?" and no person does take it, it is a battle to the cock the odds are on; but the pitter of the pounded cock has the right to have the pound put up, that is, twenty dollars against one; should not this be complied with, then the pitter shall go on as though there was no poundage.

12. If a cock is pounded and the poundage taken, and if the cock the odds are laid against should get up and knock down his adversary, then if the other cock is pounded and the poundage not taken, before the pitter counts twenty twice, and calls out "Who takes it?" three times, he wins, although there was a poundage before.

13. It shall be the duty of the respective pitters to deliver their cocks fair on their feet on the outer mark or score, facing each other, and in a standing position, except on the fifth ten being told; and also on the ninth ten being told, when they shall be placed on the centre score, breast to breast and beak to beak, in like manner. Any pitter being guilty of shoving his fowl across the score, or of pinching him, or using any other unfair means for the purpose of making his cock fight, shall lose the fight.

14. If both cocks fight together, and then   both should refuse until they are counted out, in such cases a fresh cock is to be hoveled and brought into the pit, and the pitters are to toss for which cock is to be set to first; he that wins has the choice; then the one which is to set to last is to be taken up, but not carried out of the pit. The hoveled cock is then to be put down to the other and let fight, whilst the judges, or one of them, shall count twenty and the other in like manner, and if one fight and the other refuse, it is a battle to the fighting cock; but if both fight or both refuse, it is a drawn battle.

N. B.—This rule is rarely carried into effect, but any pitter can exact it if he thinks proper to do so.

15. If both cocks refuse fighting until four, five or more, or less tens are counted, the pitters shall continue their count until one cock has refused ten times; for when a pitter begins to count, he counts for both cocks.

16. If a cock should die before they are counted out, if he fights last he wins the battle; this, however, is not to apply when his adversary is running away

17. The crowing or raising of the hackle of a cock is not fight, nor is fighting at the pitter's hands.

18. A breaking cock is a fighting cock, but a cock breaking from his adversary is not fight.

19. If any dispute arises between the pitters on the result of a fight, the cocks are not to be taken out of the pit, nor the gaffe taken off until it is decided by the judges or referee.

20. Each cock, within two ounces of each other, shall be a match; except blinkers when fighting against two-eyed cocks, an allowance from three to five ounces shall be made; when blinkers are matched against each other, the same rule to apply as to two-eyed cocks.

21. All matches must be fought with heels, round from the socket to the point, not exceeding one and a quarter inches in length, unless otherwise agreed upon. Drop Sockets, Cutters, Slashers and Twisted heels shall be considered foul.

22. Previous to heeling the cocks, in fighting mains, the four spurs, of same pattern and size, shall be placed together, and the pitters shall toss for choice of them.

23. In all mains, at the end of each battle, the judges shall order the spurs to be changed, i. e., the spurs of the winning cock to be placed on the loser's next fowl, and changed at the end of every battle.

24. Any person fighting a cock heavier than he is represented on the match list shall lose the fight, although he may have won.

25. In all cases of appeal, fighting ceases until the judges or the referee give their decision, which shall be final and strictly to the question before them.

26. When a bet is made it cannot be declared off unless by consent of both parties; all outside bets to go according to the main bet.

27. Each pitter, when delivering his cock on the score, shall take his hands off him as quickly as possible.

28. Any person violating any of the above rules shall be deemed to have lost the match.

ALBANY (N. Y.) RULES.

1. Each and every cock to be weighed before fighting, any cock exceeding the weight named, forfeits the match, two ounces always being given or taken.

2. Cocks to be shown with long hackle, with fair inch and a quarter round, low socket heels.

3. The crowing of a cock or throwing up the hackle in the hands of the handler does not denote fight.

4. The cocks to be picked and brought to the station and delivered.

5. Cocks shall not be handled while fighting.

6. The last cock showing fight is entitled to the count, which is five times ten, counted out loud when they are breasted.

7. If either cock refuses fight, after the count of ten five times in succession, after being breasted the one that had the count counts thirty, and then twenty, when the other cock is counted out.

8. When a cock is pounded and not taken, the pitter counts twenty, then asks "Who takes it?" three times, and that wins.

9. If one cock is standing on another, neither cock is to be touched while their feathers are touching—when free, if one cock is on his

back, or if his wing is away from him, the handler can put his wing under him, but not to put him on his feet.

10. The referee's decision to be final in all cases.

WESTERN NEW YORK RULES.

1. The pit shall be at least twelve feet in diameter and ten inches in height. A chalk mark in the centre, and two outer marks eighteen inches from the centre.

2. The handlers shall choose a judge to decide all matters in dispute during the fighting. In all cases of appeal the fighting ceases until the judge gives his decision, which shall be final. If any dispute arises between the pitters the cocks are not to be taken from the pit, nor the spurs taken off until it is decided by the judge.

3. Cocks within two ounces are a match, except blinkers, when three to five ounces should be allowed.

4. The spurs shall be one and a quarter inch, round head, fair from socket to point, to be changed every fight.

5. The pitters shall deliver their cocks fair on their feet on the outer mark, excepting the first scoring, which should be at least four feet from the centre score.

6. When one cock has refused to fight, the pitter of the fighting cock shall count ten clear and distinct, and appeal to the judge for a count. If allowed, he will count five tens, naming and scoring at each ten at the outer score. At the fifth ten they will breast at the centre, and the pitter of the cock that has the count shall count twenty and win the fight.

7. If during a count both cocks refuse to fight, the pitter of the cock fighting last shall be entitled to the count. The judge shall decide who is entitled to the count if both pitters claim the count.

8. If a cock fights last, he wins the fight even should he die before the count is out. A cock picking is a fighting cock, excepting on the fifth ten being told, when he must be a breaking cock to break the count. A fighting cock does not break his own count.

9. A pitter is not allowed to handle his cock after he is delivered without counting ten clear and distinct, and one cock refusing to fight. The judge shall overlook a small error, and to the best of his knowledge let the best cock win.

10. Any pitter guilty of squeezing his bird, or shoving him across the score, or taking feathers from or sucking or wiping his beak, shall be deemed foul handling, and if claimed he shall lose the fight.

11. The birds shall be weighed before leaving the pit, before or after the fight, as agreed upon. If the winner is heavier than the match list provides, he loses. Two ounces over check weight is a match.

12. The poundage shall be twenty to one. The pitter of the cock pounding shall count twenty twice, at the end of which he shall say, *Who takes?* three times. The money shall be put in the pit; if not taken he wins; if taken he shall count five tens, as usual. A cock can be pounded five times; if taken once he can pound him again,

the odds and taken money to be handed to the judge by one of the pitters.

13. A cock pounded, if he in turn has recovered, can pound the cock that the odds were first on.

14. The birds shall, if hackled, be sure to have no foul hackle.

15. A cock on his back can be turned over by his handler, but not on his side. The handler can only handle his bird without asking the judge when he is fast in himself or in the pit. The judge should say quickly, when they are fast in each other, *Handle!*

16. The judge's decision in all cases is to be final.

17. A cock running away cannot win. If both run, they shall be tried by a fresh cock; if one fights and the other does not, the fighting cock wins; if both refuse, the fight shall be declared a draw.

18. Any violation of the above rules loses the fight.

BOSTON (MASS.) RULES.

1. All fowls brought to the pit must be weighed and marked down, for those to see that have fowls to fight.

2. Fowls within two ounces are a match.

3. A stag is allowed four ounces when he fights against a cock.

4. A blinker is allowed four ounces when he fights against a sound fowl.

5. Fowls being ready, brought to pit.

6. Each man takes his station and sets his fowl to the right or left, as he pleases; there remains till the fowls are in one another, or in the tan, or on his back.

7. The handler shall not assist his fowl from where he sits him; if he does, he forfeits the battle

8. In no case shall they handle the fowls, unless they are in one another, or can count ten between fighting.

9. The fowls in hand, each man to his station; either counting ten, the fowls must be set, or the delinquent loses the match.

10. The fowls set, either refuses to show fight, the last that showed has the count, which is five times ten, and then they are breasted.

11. The fowls are breasted at every five times ten, after once being breasted.

12. The fowls brought to the breast, the one that had the count counts five times ten more, and then twenty—then he claims the battle, which is his.

13. In case the fowls show while counting, it destroys the count, and they commence again.

14. In case a fowl is on his back, his handler can turn him over.

15. In all cases the parties can select judges from the company present.

16. In no case shall any person talk with the handlers while the fowls are fighting.

17. All weighing will be left to a man selected for the purpose.

18. All matches will be fought with round heels, unless otherwise agreed upon.

19. A man known to use any other, unless agreed upon, forfeits the battle.

20. All cutters, slashers and twisted heels are barred from the pit.

21. In all cases the last fowl that shows fight has the count.

22. All fowls brought to the pit that do not show fight, do not lose the battle, unless otherwise agreed upon.

BALTIMORE (MD.) RULES.

1. All birds shall be weighed, give or take two ounces, shall be a match or otherwise, if parties see fit to make it so.

2. When a stag is matched against a cock, the stag will be entitled to four ounces advance in weight. Blinkers are allowed four ounces when fighting against two-eyed cocks.

3. The handlers shall each choose one judge, who shall choose a referee; said judges shall decide all matters in dispute during the pendency of the fight. But in case of their inability to agree, then it shall be the duty of the referee to decide, and his decision shall be final.

4. Thirty seconds (or a count of fifteen by the judge or referee, as the handlers may agree) shall be allowed between each and every round.

5. It shall be the duty of the referee to keep time between the rounds, and notify the handlers to get ready at twenty-five seconds, call time at thirty seconds, when the handlers must be prompt in piting their cocks, and if either handler refuse to do so he shall lose the fight.

6. It shall be fair for handlers to pull feathers and sling blood, or any other thing to help the bird between handlings.

7. It shall be foul for A or B to touch their birds while fighting, unless one is fast to the other, but if a bird should unfortunately fasten himself with his own heel it shall be fair to handle, but on no other consideration, and either handler violating or deviating from the above rules shall lose his fight.

8. In counting, the bird showing fight last shall be entitled to the count.

9. The handlers shall pit their birds in their respective places when time is called, and the handler having the count shall count ten, then handle two more successive times and count ten each time. When time is called again, the birds shall be placed in the centre of the pit, breast to breast and beak to beak, and twenty more counted, and if the bird not having the count refuse to fight, the one having it shall be declared the winner.

10. It shall be the duty of the respective handlers to deliver their birds fair on their feet at each pitting, on the mark or score facing each other and in a standing position.

11. A peck or blow at the opponent's bird, and not at his handler, will be considered fighting.

12. When time is called, the handlers must let go their birds from their respective places, fair and square; for it shall be foul for

either handler to pitch or toss his bird upon his opponent's, and either one violating the above rule shall lose his fight.

13. If both birds fight together, and then if both should refuse, they are to be pitted at the outer score twice, and then breasted on the centre score, breast to breast and beak to beak, in a standing position; in this case the birds are to lay in the pit thirty seconds at each pitting, and at the last pitting, if both should refuse, it is a drawn battle.

14. In the case of a bird that dies, if he fights last and his handler has the count he wins the battle.

15. Whenever a bird is fast in his adversary, the handler of the bird the spurs are fast in shall draw them out, but the handler of a bird has no right to draw out his own spur except when fast in himself, or in the floor, or in the web of the pit.

16. The greasing, peppering or soaping a cock, or any other external applications, are unfair practices, and by no means admissible in this amusement.

17. The handlers are to give the birds room to fight, and not to hover and press on them so as to retard their striking.

18. Any person fighting a bird heavier than he is represented on the match list, shall lose the fight although he may have won.

19. In all cases of appeal, fighting ceases until the judges, or the referee, give their decision, which shall be final and strictly to the question before them.

20. Each handler, when delivering his bird on the score, shall take his hands off him as quickly as possible.

21. No handler shall touch his bird unless at the times mentioned in the foregoing rules.

22. If any dispute arises between the handlers on the result of the fight, the birds are not to be taken out of the pit, nor the gaffs taken off until it is decided by the judges or referee.

23. It shall be the duty of the judges and referee to watch all movements of the fights, and judge according to the above rules.

24. When a bet is made it cannot be declared off unless by consent of both parties, all outside bets to go according to the main bet.

25. Any person violating any of the above rules shall be deemed to have lost the match.

VIRGINIA OR SOUTHERN RULES.

ARTICLE 1. On the morning the main is to commence, the parties decide by lot who shows first. It is to be remembered that the party obtaining choice generally chooses to weigh first, and, consequently, obliges the adverse party to show first, as the party showing first weighs last. When the show is made by the party, the door of the cock house is to be locked, and the key given to the other party, who immediately repairs to his cock house and prepares for weighing. There ought to be provided a pair of good scales, and weights as low down as half an ounce. One or two judges to be appointed to weigh the cocks. Each party, by weighing the cocks intended for the show a day or two beforehand, and having all their respective weights, would greatly facilitate the

business of the judges.   There should be two writers to take
down the colors, weights, marks, &c., of each cock.   There ought
to be no feathers cut or plucked from the cocks before they are
brought to the scale, except a few from behind to keep them
clean, and their wings and tail clipped a little.

2. As soon as the cocks are all weighed, the judge, the writers
and principals of each party, and as many besides as the parties
may agree on, are to retire for the purpose of matching.   They
are to make all even matches first, then those within one ounce,
and afterwards those within two ounces; but if more matches can
be made by breaking an even or one ounce match, it is to be
done.

3. On the day of the showing only one battle is to be fought.
It is to be remembered that the party winning the show gains
also the choice of fighting this first battle with any particular
cocks in the match; afterwards they begin with the lightest pair
first, and so on up to the heaviest, fighting them in rotation, as
they increase in weight.   This first battle, too, will fix the mode
of trimming.

RULES TO BE OBSERVED ON THE PIT.

1. When the cocks are on the pit, the judges are to examine
whether they answer the description taken in the match bill,
and whether they are fairly trimmed and have on fair heels.   If all
be right and fair, the pitters are to deliver their cocks six feet
apart (or thereabouts), and retire a step or two back; but if a
wrong cock should be produced, the party so offending forfeits that
battle.

2. All heels that are round from the socket to the point are allowed to be fair; any pitter bringing a cock on the pit with any
other kind of heels, except by particular agreement, forfeits the
battle.

3. If either cock should be trimmed with a close, unfair hackle,
the judge shall direct the other to be cut in the same manner; and
at that time shall observe to the pitter that if he brings another
cock in the like situation, unless he shall have been previously
trimmed, he shall forfeit the battle.

4. A pitter, when he delivers his cock, shall retire two paces back,
and not advance or walk round his cock, until a blow is passed.

5. An interval of ten minutes shall be allowed between the
termination of one battle and the commencement of another.

6. No pitter shall pull a feather out of a cock's mouth, nor from
over his eyes or head, or pluck him by the breast, to make him
fight, or pinch him for the like purpose, under penalty of forfeiting
the battle.

7. The pitters are to give their cocks room to fight, and are not to
hover or press on them, so as to retard them from striking.

8. Greasing, peppering, muffing and soaping a cock, or any other
external application, are unfair practices, and by no means admissible in this amusement.

9. The judge, when required, may suffer a pitter to call in a few
of his friends to assist in catching his cock, who are to retire im-

mediately as soon as the cock is caught, and in no other instance is the judge to suffer the pit to be broken.

10. All cocks on their backs are to be immediately turned over on their bellies, by their respective pitters, at all times.

11. A cock, when down, is to have a wing given to him, if he needs it, unless his adversary is on it, but his pitter is to place the wing gently in its proper position, and not to lift the cock, and no wing is to be given unless absolutely necessary.

12. If either cock should be hanged in himself, in the pit or canvas, he is to be loosed by his pitter, but if in his adversary, both pitters are immediately to lay hold of their respective cocks, and the pitter whose cock is hung shall hold him steadily whilst the adverse party draws out the heel, and then they shall take their cocks asunder a sufficient distance for them fairly to renew the combat.

13. Should the cocks separate, and the judge be unable to decide which fought last, he shall, at his discretion, direct the pitters to carry their cocks to the middle of the pit, and deliver them beak to beak, unless either of them is blind, in which case they are to be shouldered; that is, delivered with their breasts touching, each pitter taking care to deliver his cock at this, as well as at all other times, with one hand.

14. When both cocks cease fighting, it is then in the power of the pitter of the last fighting cock, unless they touch each other, to demand a count of the judge, who shall count 40 deliberately, which, when counted out, is not to be counted again during the battle. Then the pitters shall catch their cocks, and carry them to the middle of the pit, and deliver them beak to beak, but to be shouldered if either of them is blind, as before. Then, if either cock refuses or neglects to fight, the judge shall count ten, and shall call out "once refused," and shall direct the pitters to bring their cocks again to the middle of the pit, and put to as before; and if the same cock in like manner refuses, shall count ten again and call out "twice refused," and so proceed until one cock thus refuses 6 times successively. The judge shall then determine the battle against such cock.

15. If either cock die before the judge can finish the counting of the law, the battle is to be given to the living cock, and if both die the longest liver wins the battle.

16. The pitters are not to touch their cocks whilst the judge is in the act of counting.

17. No pitter is ever to lay hold of his adversary's cock unless to draw out the heel, and then he must take him below the knee. Then there shall be no second delivery; that is, after he is once delivered, he shall not be touched until a blow is struck, unless ordered by the judge.

18. No pitter shall touch his cock, unless at the times mentioned in the foregoing rules.

19. If any pitter acts contrary to these rules, the judge, if called on at the time, shall give the battle against him.

NEW ORLEANS (LA.) RULES.

1. All birds shall be weighed; give or take two ounces shall be a match or otherwise, if parties see fit to make it so.

2. All heels to be fought with, shall be round from socket to a point, or as near so as can be made.

3. When a stag is matched against a cock the stag will be entitled to four ounces advance in weight.

4. It shall be fair for handlers to pull feathers and sling blood, or any other thing to help the bird between handlings.

5. It shall be foul for A or B to touch their birds while fighting, unless one is fast to the other, but if a bird should unfortunately fasten himself with his own heel, it shall be fair to handle, but on no other consideration, and either handler violating or deviating from the above rule shall lose his fight.

6. Thirty seconds shall be allowed between each and every round.

7. In counting, the bird showing fight last shall be entitled to the count, but if his handler refuse to take the count, the opposite handler shall be entitled to it.

8. The handler having the count shall pit his bird in his respective place when time is called, and count ten, then handle three more successive times; when time is called again the birds shall be placed in the centre of the pit, breast to breast, and forty more counted, and if the bird not having the count refuse to fight, the one having it shall be declared the winner.

9. A peck or blow at the opponent's bird, and not at his handler, will be considered fighting.

10. When time is called, the handlers must let go their birds from their respective places, fair and square, for it shall be foul for either handler to pitch or toss his bird upon his opponent's, and either one violating the above rule shall lose his fight.

11. Each party shall choose a judge, and the judges choose a disinterested party as a referee. No referee will be competent who has bet on either side, or is otherwise interested.

12. It shall be the duty of the judges and referee to watch all movements of the fight, and judge according to the above rules. The referee will be confined to the opinions of the judges only, and his decision is final.

13. It shall be the duty of the referee to keep time between the rounds and notify the handlers to get ready at twenty-five seconds, then call time at thirty seconds, when the handlers must be prompt in pitting their birds, and if either handler refuse to do so, he shall lose his fight.

DETROIT (MICH.) RULES.

Rule 1. All birds shall be weighed. Give or take two oz. shall be a match.

2. When a stag is matched against a cock, the stag shall be allowed five ounces the advantage.

3. All birds shall be cut out and deprived of their hackle or glossy feathers.

4. Gaffs, spurs or heels must be round from socket to point.

5. It shall be fair for handlers to pull feathers and sling blood.

6. It shall be foul for A or B to touch their birds while fighting, unless one is fast to the other. But if a cock should unfortunately

fasten himself with his own heels, it shall be fair to handle, but on no other consideration, and either handler violating or deviating from the above rule shall lose his fight.

7. The longest liver, when both cocks are mortally wounded, shall be declared the winner.

8. Thirty seconds shall be allowed between each and every round.

9. In counting, the bird showing fight last shall be entitled to the count, but if the handler does not take the count, the opposite handler shall be entitled to take it.

10. The handler having the count shall count ten and pit his bird in his respective place, and count ten again, and so on until he has counted forty, then the birds must be piled breast to breast, and he must count forty, and the battle is over unless the opposite bird shows fight by making a peck, which breaks the count, and the fight proceeds.

11. When time is called the handlers must let go their birds from their respective places fair and square, for it shall be foul for either handler to toss or pitch his bird upon his opponent's, and either violating the above rule shall lose the fight.

12. Each party shall choose a judge, and the judge shall choose a disinterested person, who shall be styled the referee. No person shall be considered competent to act as referee if it be known that he has bet one cent, more or less, on the match or matches.

13. It shall be the duty of the judges to watch the motions of the handlers, and, if anything foul occurs, they must appeal to the referee, and his decision must be final; however, it will be the duty of the referee to notice all complaints from the judges only, and, after due consideration, his decision must be given in strict accordance with the above rules.

14. It shall be the duty of the referee to call time between the rounds, and at the call of time the handlers must be prompt, and if either handler refuses to obey he shall lose his fight.

SAN FRANCISCO (CAL.) RULES.

1. When the cocks are brought to the pit the pitters enter the same, and no other person or persons shall be admitted within its limits. The pitters then proceed to examine the cocks and see that they have on fair heels. Secondly, that neither of the parties have resorted to the unmanly and foul practice of greasing, soaping, peppering, or making any other external application, all of which are foul and inadmissible.

2. All things being right and fair, the pitters shall deliver their cocks fairly on their feet upon the score, and then retire one or two steps, and not move their hands or walk around their cocks until a blow is struck, then they may approach their cocks for the purpose of handling them when they hang, but they are not to hover over the cocks so as to retard or prevent them from making a blow, and if either cock refuses to make fight, it shall then be considered no match.

3. When the cocks are banged the pitters shall lay hold of their

respective cocks, and the party whose cock is hanged shall hold him steadily while the reverse party draws the heel, nor shall either party cause, in any manner, unnecessary injury or punishment while the heels are being extracted, and as soon as the cocks are freed they shall again be delivered on the score.

4. All cocks hanged in the canvas, ground, or in themselves, shall be loosened by their respective pitters at all times.

5. When one or both cocks are hanged, it is necessary to handle them and deliver them at the score, so they may renew the combat fairly.

6. When the cocks are put to, if either cock refuses to fight, the other pitter has a right to the count, when he proceeds to count forty deliberately, which, when counted, is not to be counted again during that battle.

7. Should either or both cocks, after being delivered, not make fight, the pitter whose cock fought last shall be entitled to the count, when he shall count deliberately six times ten, and at every count they shall both handle and deliver their cocks on the score. On the third and sixth count they shall deliver their cocks breast to breast, and if on the sixth count, after being so delivered, they do not make fight, the pitter having the count shall have won the fight.

8. If in counting the law the other cock makes fight, that breaks the count, and if he is the last fighter he is entitled to the count; but one must refuse or neglect to make fight six successive times before the battle can be decided against him.

9. If either or both cocks die before the pitters finish counting the law, the fight shall be awarded to the last fighting cock.

10. Neither pitter shall be allowed to touch or handle his cock while counting the law.

11. No pitter shall be allowed to suck or sling blood from his cock's throat or mouth, nor pluck feathers from over his eyes or out of his mouth.

12. All cocks lying on their backs shall be turned on their bellies by their respective pitters, at all times, provided the other cock is not standing on him. If his pitter neglect or refuse to turn him, it is then admissible for the other pitter to turn him gently on his belly.

13. All cocks shall have a wing given them, provided the other is not upon it. In giving the wing it is to be placed gently by his side, without raising the cock or helping him on his feet.

14. When both cocks break together, and the pitters and judges are unable to decide which fought last, or when both are hanged in each other, it shall be the duty of the judges to order them to the score; then if both refuse to fight, the pitters shall count the law, and have them put to as if the count were actually going on; and if neither make fight before the count is finished the fight shall be pronounced drawn.

15. Any pitter acting contrary to the foregoing rules forfeits the battle.

CANADIAN RULES.

RULE 1. All birds shall be *weighed*, give or take two ounces, shall be a match or otherwise, if parties see fit to make it so.

2. All heels to be fought with *shall be round*, from socket to point, or as near as can be made.

3. When a stag is matched against a cock, the stag will be entitled to four ounces advance in weight.

4. It shall be fair for handlers to pull feathers and sling blood, or any other thing to help the bird between handlings.

5. It shall be foul for A or B to touch their birds while fighting, unless one is fast to the other, but if a bird should unfortunately *fasten himself* with his own heel, *it shall be fair to handle*, but on no other consideration, and either handler violating or deviating from the above rule shall lose his fight.

6. Thirty seconds shall be allowed before each and every round.

7. In counting, the bird showing fight last shall be entitled to the count, but if his handler refuses to take the count, the opposite handler shall be entitled to it.

8. The handler having the count shall pit his bird in his respective place *when time is called*, and count ten, then handle three more successive times; when time is called again, the birds shall be placed in the centre of the pit, *breast to breast*, and forty more counted, and if the bird not having the count refuses to fight, the one having it shall be declared the winner.

9. A peck or blow at the opponent's bird, and not at his handler, will be considered fighting.

10. When time is called the handlers must let go their birds from their respective places, *fair and square*, for it shall be *foul* for either handler to pitch or toss his bird upon his opponent's, and either one violating the above rule shall lose his fight.

11. Each party shall choose a judge, and the judges choose a *disinterested party* as a referee. No referee will be competent who has bet on either side, or is otherwise interested.

12. It shall be the duty of the judges and referee to watch all movements of the fight, and judge according to the above rules. The referee will be confined to the opinions of the judges only, *and his decision final.*

13. It shall be the duty of the referee to *keep time* between the rounds, and notify the handlers to get ready at *twenty-five seconds*, then call *time* at *thirty seconds*, when the handlers must be prompt in pitting their birds; and if either handler refuses to do so, he shall lose his fight.

ROYAL COCK PIT RULES of WESTMINSTER, ENG.

1. That every person show and put his cock into the pit with a fair hackle, not too near shorn, or out, nor with any other fraud.

2. That every cock fight as he is first shown in the pit, without shearing or cutting any feathers afterward, except with the consent of both the masters of the match.

3. When both cocks are set down to fight, and one of them runs away before they have struck three mouthing blows, it is adjudged no battle to the persons who bet.

4. No person to set-to but those who are appointed by the masters of the match.

5. When a cock shall come setting-to, and both cocks refuse to fight ten times successively according to law, then a fresh cock shall be hoveled, and the masters of the match must agree which of them shall turn the cock down;·after that, if both fight, or both refuse, to be deemed a drawn battle; but if one should fight, and the other refuse, the battle to be allowed won by the fighting cock.

6. After the person appointed by the masters to tell the law shall have told twice twenty, the cocks to be set-to, beak to beak if they both see, but if either be blind, then the blind cock to touch; and on their refusing to fight, the person appointed as before is to tell ten between each setting-to, till one of the cocks has refused to fight ten times successively.

7. When ten pounds to a crown are laid on the battle, and not taken, after twice twenty is told, the battle is determined as won by that cock the odds are on.

8. That no person shall make any cavil or speech about matching of cocks, either to matchers or owners, after the cocks are once put together.

9. A master of a match has a right to remove any person out of the lower ring.

10. No person can make a confirmed bet void without mutual consent.

11. Bets to be paid on clear proof by creditable witnesses, even though they have not been demanded immediately after the battle is over.

12. It is recommended that all disputes be finally determined by the masters of the match, and two other gentlemen whom they shall appoint; and in case the four cannot agree, then they shall fix on a fifth, whose determination shall be final.

MODERN
SYSTEM OF BREEDING.

Since the GAME COCK was first published we have received the ILLUSTRATED BOOK OF POULTRY, published in England, and select therefrom the following very excellent remarks on the modern system of breeding, etc., from the pen of Mr. John Harris, of Liskeard, Cornwall, a gentleman of over forty years' experience.

The law that "like produces like," is only true if the birds are of a pure and known blood, and this is the great secret in breeding. For color we chiefly look to the hen in Game, and to the cock for style and symmetry; but the most wonderful point is the suddenness with which any change of cocks in a run will change the blood and apparently reverse this rule. I have proved this by setting the fourth egg after change, having put a Brown-red to Black-red hens, taking away the same evening the Black-red cock. The fourth egg produced a splendidly colored Brown-red cockerel; and wonderful to say, from one hen of pure Black-red blood I thus obtained nine Brown-reds and not one Black-red. Nevertheless, the rule will generally hold good of depending on the hen for color. The

selfsame hen, two years before, when a pullet, was left
without a mate after the first two eggs were laid, and
every egg of the batch produced a good Black-red. This
is the mystery how suddenly the influence of one cock
seems destroyed by the introduction of another in the run;
and there is no way of proving this so well as breeding the
different colors in Game.

As an instance of how birds with any admixture of
blood will retain it and "throw back," even after twenty
years have passed, I may mention the following:—A
short, very hard-feathered spangled cock having been put
to a Black-red hen, a cockerel from this cross, put to the
mother, threw some of the finest Black-reds ever seen in
England. A cockerel from this cross, put to the hens of
the first cross, gave a second family, which were bred
backwards and forwards as required, and kept the color
well for twelve years. At the end of this time a cockerel
and pullets being mated of the same hatch, produced a
few Spangles, which were shown and won the first prize
in the "Any Variety" class of Game at Birmingham.
Again, nine years later, by putting together a cockerel and
pullets from the same hatch, and from the same blood, I
had a still greater number of Spangles come out. This
retention of the cross being so remarkable, I thought it
worth mentioning, especially as the difference in color
being so great there was no mistaking it; and it shows
how careful we ought to be, after putting together different
colors, to keep it from reappearing when not wanted.

One very mistaken notion is the idea of most breeders
as to the few hens they think ought to be put to a cock.
Just keep in mind how many prolific eggs you will get
from a hen after the cock has been taken away, and consider in that time, even if twenty hens had been running
with the cock, whether during the length of time she would
have been in laying trim—say while she laid eleven eggs—
the cock would not have paid attention to each of those
twenty, and the eggs be far more likely to produce strong
chickens? I have proof, and very strong proof, even in
heavy birds; for the most successful year I ever had in
Dorkings I ran seventeen hens with one cockerel, and never had I such heavy and strong-constitutioned birds.
Feed well, and give a good run, and I should not be afraid
to run twenty-five hens with one cock, though he must be
a young healthy bird; but even a two-year-old I should

not fear to mate with eleven hens, and would expect to be successful.

Game hens, on the whole, are good average layers, and there are no better mothers for protecting the chickens. I have seen a Game hen with chickens drive off all sorts of enemies, from a horse to a rat, and I have seen a Game hen actually kill a rat, a rook, and even a hawk ; nothing is so big or savage but that she will defend her brood from it. In general I put eleven eggs under each hen. Unless a few hens hatch off the same day, we are obliged to set the coops far apart, or destruction would be the result. The best time to get Game hatched is from the middle of March to the end of April. Get them to nice cottage-runs as early as possible after they leave the hens ; and, if this is not convenient, divide pullets and cockerels—it will save many a fight. Dub as you find walks for them.

REARING.

A few hints as to rearing will not be out of place to those who may be about starting. Never put more than eleven eggs under a Game hen. When hatched be in no hurry to take them from the nest, for they will want nothing for twenty-four hours, and very little then; and as you should feed the first two or three days with egg custard and a few dry crumbs of bread mixed with the custard, they will require no water; so put none near for them to dabble in. In a day or two take the hen from where she has hatched to a dry shed facing the south, or a dry bank sheltered from north and east winds, and coop them on the ground. If too wet put some dry ashes under the coop, soft and free from lumps, and by no means put them on boards, for by this we get crooked toes; and rough cinders or gravel sometimes indent the small gristle of the breast, and if it gets the least askew while with the hen, it soon goes worse and worse. Some breeders say they have had them come straight, but this is doubtful. Let your coop remain four or five days at first, by merely drawing the hen's droppings out. When you do shift, do so at midday, and if damp or wet put more dry ashes or dry earth at night. You will find fussing about this dry lodging pay for the trouble, by seeing your chickens come out quite frisky in the morning, and it conduces greatly to health.

Coop the hens for six or seven weeks with the chicks, feeding principally on egg custard, coarse oatmeal, and bruised wheat until about five weeks old, then give well-soaked whole wheat a few times daily, weaning them off to the common food by degrees. It is very useful, if there is no old hedge or low trees near by where your coops are placed, to drive four stakes in the ground, standing about a foot high, and place a hurdle on them, then lay a few loose boughs on it. This serves as a playground in a cold morning, as they soon commence to fly up and down after one another; then again, before the earth gets warm for their feet, they will cluster on the top of it when the sun comes out, and preen themselves. It makes a nice break between the coops, and is a protection as well, for if there should be any large bird on the wing they are under in a moment. Do not let them roost until about three months old if you can help it, so that you have plenty of soft clean stuff to let them sleep on. They keep warmer in a heap, and grow stronger, and it establishes a stronger constitution. Use sulphate of iron in the water and your fowl will never have the gapes or roup. The egg custard is made as follows:—Beat three eggs up in half a pint of new milk, put in a saucepan, and stir over the fire until it becomes a thick curd; then press the whey out by squeezing in a cloth. Give this custard every morning, and as they get older mix oatmeal and ground rice, which forms a very nutritious food, and they will grow and thrive on it wonderfully. The great effect of custard thus fed, to the chickens getting the rich and strengthening diet the first thing every morning, and it is digested quicker than any other. If sulphate of iron is in the water, it is not requisite to change it so often as it would be if pure water.

DUBBING GAME.

The age for dubbing is in general seventeen or eighteen weeks old. Dubbing, it need hardly be said, is the removal of comb, wattles, and ear-lobes. To do this properly, so as to cause the least loss of blood, the cock should be held by an assistant by the thigh and shoulder of the wing, pressing the bird close to his breast with one hand, while with the other he lays hold of the comb, keeping the bird with his head and breast slightly turned up. The operator then lays hold of the wattle, (the fleshy excrescence that grows under the throat) inserting the point of his dubbing scissors at the lower mandible, or jaw, and striking straight for the ear, leaving the old skin about half an inch, or hardly so much, between your cut and the eye. When you get to the ear commence again at the under side of the wattle, and run the point of the scissors about half way down, then dissect gradually up to the ear. I have often taken the wattles off in this way without losing a salt-spoonful of blood from both wattles. When wattles and ears are off, the assistant takes the cockerel well in hand by the shoulders and thighs, when the operator inserts his left thumb across the inside of the beak, placing his forefinger at the back of the head. Care must, however, be taken not to choke the bird. Then setting his scissors close and firmly on the head, straight up from the beak, with one cut, by keeping the scissors well pressed down as he cuts he will take the comb clean off; then merely a slight cut each side of the beak, to take off a small excrescence that would make the setting in at the beak heavy, and the operation is over, and, if convenient, the cock may be tossed up in the air. The blood usually stops at once, and nothing more is required. He will then be nice and red again in six weeks, and fit to exhibit.

PREPARING GAME FOR SHOW.

The preparation necessary to fit Game fowls for show. First of all, when taken off their walks to pen for a day or two, before sending off to show, gently sponge the head and face with some lukewarm water and soap, then their legs and feet. When thoroughly dry, get your attendant to hold the cock firmly but gently, the hands round the thighs, and his thumbs on the shoulder-coverts, the thumb not pressed in, but to feel and be ready to press if the cock should attempt to struggle; the operation then commences, by putting the left hand swiftly round the cock's head and neck, and running the scissors straight from the back of the comb to the beak, taking all the little spike-like feathers off close, which gives the head a much smoother and finer appearance; then draw the skin sideways off the cheek, tight, with the thumb, and carry the scissors along the cheek in the same way, which will smooth all the little spiky feathers off there. Many draw them out with small pincers, but we do not approve of this, as it has to be repeated, but when close clipped it is done with. All that is left to be done is with a small, nice, clean sponge, and a very little salad oil, to sponge the fleshy parts of the head and face, but not leaving a lot of oil on; this is what gives the nice, bright, coral-like appearance that most professional show men's Game have their first day in the show pens.

A Game cock, if well walked, requires no feeding to prepare for the show; but, if in low condition, about three or four days in a quite clean pen, feeding twice a day on a teacupful of nice boiled new milk and bread, with a handful of thoroughly good barley at night, will make a great difference, and throw a nice gloss on the feathers. This is all that is necessary, for it does not answer to train a cock for show as you would to fight If living handy to his run, it is well to give a feed of split peas daily for a fortnight; but a naturally hard-fleshed bird, taken off his walk, may be fed on almost what you like. A cock for fighting is got up to a certain pitch just by a certain day, after which he goes back fast; but that would not do for show. A cock should be shown as nearly in his natural condition as possible; but if fed up for showing he will show it the second day.

To keep them right on returning from shows, give boiled milk and bread, but no hard food, for the first day or so; then feed as usual, when, if of good constitution, they will be fit again in a week's time. For several weeks they will keep this up without perceptible injury; as, having no extra flesh to carry, like Cochins, they can stand it better.

GAME AS LAYERS AND EATING.

Most Game hens are excellent layers, averaging as high as 200 eggs per annum on a good range; but other varieties fall far short of this. All Game fowls, however, if killed moderately young, are the choicest eating possible. They will not bear fattening; but if taken up just as they are, after good feeding, are almost like the pheasant in quality of flesh. Merely as a table fowl, the larger strains of hen-feathered Game would be preferable, as cocks may easily be bred reaching nearly eight pounds, and

by breeding young birds together the highest quality of
meat may be obtained.   From lack of feathers, Game
fowls are deceiving as to the weight of meat they carry.
Compared with most other poultry they look small; but
on taking them up it is found that they are larger than
they look, and that they feel almost "like lead" in the
hand.   When, therefore, they can be allowed free range
round the country house, with space sufficient to prevent
much fighting, they are an advantageous breed to keep.

HOW TO KEEP ORDER AMONG CHICKENS.

Game chickens are certainly very tiresome to manage.
The quarrelsome disposition shows itself at a very early
age; and we have known a bird fight till its windpipe was
torn open, long before it was fully fledged.   Even the
little pullets will often fight freely, but their quarrels rarely produce much harm.   As they will generally live peace-
ably enough after the mastery is once thoroughly decided,
many breeders get over the difficulty by buffeting with a
bag or handkerchief what seem to be the weaker birds,
thus hastening the victory of the stronger ones; after
which, for a time at least, the trouble is over.   Temporary
separation is not of the slighest use, only making the
fighting worse than ever when the little sinners are allowed
to meet again; once the quarrelling begins, it must be decided before peace can be re-established.   Later on, when
the chicks are old enough to be separated and live apart
from the hen, there is much less difficulty, as the cockerels may be put up together with a strong old cock who
will keep order.   It is very strange that this should be the
case with so combative a breed; but it has been proved
again and again that a good old Game cock will not allow
young ones to fight in his presence, but will walk up and
stop them, administering severe punishment if his com-
mands be disregarded.   In this way the walk may be
preserved in peace for a considerable time, so long as any
sight of hen or pullet be sedulously guarded against: but
this event is invariably followed by an obstinate fight, in
which most of the birds will be killed; and harmony can
never afterwards be re-established.   It is also necessary to
separate each stag as he is dubbed; otherwise he is always
attacked, his companions not appearing to recognize him
when shorn of the appendages thus removed.

OLD SYSTEM OF MATING.

As to the number of hens allowed to one cock. It is quite certain that amongst the old cock fighters it was an accepted rule not to place more than three or four hens with one cock, and they always considered that, for their special purposes, a greater number led to deterioration; and in those days such anxious attention was bestowed on every detail, that some may be slow to accept so total a reversal of all their ideas. Much must depend upon the birds, and much upon the range: for it is a well-proved fact that with unlimited range double the number of hens may be allowed, with even more vigor than the smaller number in a close yard. Different stock-birds, also, differ totally in their vigor and disposition; and there is not the slightest doubt that in many cases the produce has been actually weakened, and hens even rendered entirely barren, by want of sufficient mates for a very lively bird; soil, food, range, individual character, and age of the bird, with other circumstances, should be carefully weighed, and the result of experience noted in different cases before the breeder proceeds to form any rule for his own guidance.

DESCRIPTION OF GAME
AND BEST METHODS OF CROSSING.

BLACK-BREASTED RED GAME.

The points a really good Black-red cock ought to have for a stock bird should be as follows:—Beak strong, slightly curved, and stout where set on the head. Head rather inclined to be long, and not round and bullet-shaped; the least possible indent over the eye gives a snake-like appearance which is much admired. Eyes bright red, rather prominent, with a fearless expression. Face a smooth fine skin; the throat the same. Ears red, not inclined to white. Neck rather long, and a little arched; short hackle, with the points just meeting between the shoulders, but reaching very little on the back. Back flat, wide at shoulders, and narrowing to the tail. Breast round and full. Stern to be clear between the hocks, not let down, but a clear line. Saddle-feathers close and short, and not too many of them. Wings strong, and not over long, having a great substance at the shoulders; not confined close at the breast, but to be seen a little detached, as if ready to fly at the first intruder—be he cat, dog, or cock—the points resting over the thighs, but under the saddle. Tail medium length, neither too long nor short, but nicely carried; neither "squirrel" nor drooping, but between the two; not much spread out, but nicely "Venetianed," with about seven secondary sickle-feathers each side, the one nicely fitting just above the other; of course the two main sickles about four or five inches longer than the straight tail. Thighs round, stout, full of muscle, firm, rather long, but well carried in close to the body—not stilty, but so that you can distinguish their form and where set in when facing you. Shanks medium length, nicely rounded, neither flat nor quite round, with a nice clean joint in setting-on to the thigh-bone, well standing apart, and beautifully scaled. Spurs set low, and inclined to point back. Feet flat; toes well spread out, and the hind toe to come straight and flat from the foot; not as many do, drooping so as to just put the point to the ground.

This latter form is nearly as objectionable as what is termed duck-footed, which is when the hind toe inclines to point forward the same way as the front toes. The toes should be a good length, and well spread out, with good strong nails. The color of the legs should be willow or olive, to blend well with the color of this cock.

Plumage as follows:—Head and neck-hackles orange-red to the points; back and shoulder-coverts violet-red, with a shade of orange; saddle orange-red; breast black, with a steel-blue shade all over the breast; tail rich black, with a slight purple bronze shade in secondary sickles. There are different shades in the Black-reds, but none blend better, or is warmer, and nicer, and pleasanter to the eye than the above colors, which we will call No. 1 The color of another very successful shade of Black-reds, which is easier bred, but not so beautiful, we will call No. 2. The cock is more of a red clay-color in hackle, deep rich red; back and shoulder-coverts a little violet-red; the saddle similar to hackle; in fact, too much of a sameness all over to make the color pleasant, but still they have the symmetry of the more favored colored ones. There is also another color of Black-red, but it seldom proves success-ful unless a poor lot happens to be exhibited at poultry shows. The hackle is red, darkly striped, running off to light straw; back claret; shoulder-coverts red clay-color; saddle almost a red-straw. These we will call No. 3; they are in general soft to the touch for want of muscle, and far from firm in the hand.

So far as the cocks in the Black-reds are concerned, enough may be gleaned from these remarks to assist a novice, as this is intended for such, as well as reference to be compared by older hands, in breeding from what they may have. The three colors and style of hens found most useful in all our crossing to get what we want for show pur-pose in color, beginning with style and symmetry, which will do for all three useful colors, or shades of color, as all are really one. Beak to be stout where set on the head, curved slightly and sharp at the point; upper mandible same color all over, viz., dark horn; comb small, thin, straight, and evenly serrated; head rather long, neat, and snake-like; eyes red and prominent, with a fiery expres-sion; face bright red, and thin; deaf-ear red and small; wattles thin and neatly rounded; neck inclined to be long slightly curved, and short-feathered, the feathers meeting

at a point between the shoulder when the neck is extended, and not so long as to form a tippet; back in shape similar to the cock, but in the old hen inclined to be rather more broad and flat, tapering off to the tail; wings not inclined to be long, but to seem cut short in body, and powerfully made—as these are not birds meant for continual flight, they are not so long in comparison as in birds of passage, but have very strong butts and rather short pinion or flight-feathers. The wings should be carried rather high, and close in to sides. Tail moderate in length, and nicely "Venetianed," that is, each feather lapping a little over the other, like a Venetian blind, to give it a nice, neat, compact form, not open and fan-shaped. The hen should carry it a little above the horizontal line. Breast broad and prominent; thigh-bone inclined to be long, but well kept close along the body, and not stilty, with great muscle, feeling firm in the hand, so that when you have her in your hand she well fills it up. Shank clean, and scales smooth; a moderate length of bone, finishing off with good, flat, wide-spread toes; the hinder one coming out level from the foot. Carriage upright, neat, quick and active.

The color of Black-red hens is as follows:—Head and neck golden, streaked with black, but not the gold and black run into each other; body-color partridge, or as near to a partridge-color as possible, even to run up the outside or top-feathers of the tail; salmon-red breast, commencing under the throat, running off a little to ashy color on the thighs, without the least pencilling on flight-feathers in the wing. This being the principal and proper exhibition color, we will call it No. 1. The partridge-marking ought on no account to run into any distinct pencilling, though it is sometimes described as such. It is a very small, wavy, irregular marking, just like that on the back of a partridge. We do often see real pencilling, and it is difficult to breed birds without; but such marking is the greatest curse of a yard, and so often a sign of a Duck-wing or Pile cross that it ought to be more discouraged than it is. The true and proper marking is as figured here, just like a partridge, and should be so described.

The second color of hen for breeding purposes is:— Hackle golden yellow, streaked with black; body—at least back and saddle—partridge color of a Weedon or slight creamy tinge, but still partridge; the wings slightly ruddy; breast a red salmon, running off to ashy color on the thighs. This hen is of lighter shade, in fact, all over the body, a softer yellow color pervading; but the partridge-marking just the same in character as the No. 1.

The third color for.breeding is:—Head and hackle light gold, only slightly streaked with black; back and wings quite a light partridge, with a more even shade of gold all over; breast a yellowish ash-color; tail black.

Either of these colors having the style and symmetry named can be bred from, and with success; but I don't say the first cross. Put a No. 1 cock with a clear partridge-colored (or No. 1) hen, clear in the wing, and with no pencilling whatever on the flights of the wing; having a deep salmon-colored breast, with rich golden hackle, with a deep streak of black in each feather. By thus mating you would get rare pullets, and sometimes a first rate cockerel.

Then again, put No. 1 cock to a rich partridge-backed hen, with ruddy wings, and rich golden hackle streaked with rich black, and a ruddy-ashy breast, described above as No. 2. Thence you get your bright-red, showy cocker-erels; but seldom a good pullet, not being dark enough.

From No. 2 cock, being more a self-color, and not that blending of reds that is so pleasing in No. 1, you will get your rich partridge-colored hens, with deep rich salmon breasts, and pretty free from pencilling, if mated with good partridge hens. Putting this cock to a red partridge (or No. 3) hen, inclined to "wheaten" color, you sometimes get a really beautiful bright red cockerel.

With regard to No. 3 cock, the only thing I have seen his color get good has been pullets from the clear partridge (or No. 1) hens; the cockerels in general are loose-feath-ered, and too dark.

There is also what is termed the Wheaten-red hen—that is, a hen with buff breast; back slightly partridge, marked with buffy-red; hackle buff, striped with black, and tail black, inclined to be tinged with buff. The name was given from the skin of the red wheat. These hens are most valuable to a breeder for getting him a really pure bright-red cock, for which you put to them a cock of the No. 2 color; but this has to be carefully done. It is very well to use one cross, either with the bright-red, or No. 2 cock; but if you cross with the Wheaten the second time you will get a blotchy breast and rusty fluff, the blood being too light to have too much of. These hens are also useful for breeding Piles and Duckwings as mentioned farther on; but the second cross, from hens bred from the Wheaten hen, has a certain softness of feather not desirable; therefore, all Black-red hens bred from this cross ought to be cooked. It is from the second cross the softness comes, the Wheaten hen herself being hard-feathered and generally throwing very sound-feathered cockerels.

Black-reds being the purest-feathered of the Reds, I have given them the preference in describing them.

BROWN-BREASTED RED GAME.

The same description of style and symmetry as the Black-reds will do for all Game, including Brown-breasted Red Game. There are several colors admissible for poultry shows. In the streaky or starling-breasted cock, the head and hackle-feathers are deep orange-red, with a shade of dark in centre of feather; shoulder-coverts dark crimson; saddle a red maroon on centre, passing to a dark lemon and straw; breast dark, with a bay streak in centre of every feather running off on the thighs, which are also streaked with bay; tail black, sickles narrow and whip-like, and bronzed with a greenish gloss. Some like a dark smutty face, instead of the red-purple skin. Large brown or black eyes are necessary to this breed. In Brown-reds a little heavier build does not detract from the beauty of the bird, so more laxity may be taken in this color than the Black-red; but the same rule as to style applies here as to Black-reds. The Brown-reds have a hardness of feather that few strains of the Black-reds possess.

The color of hen to match the streaky-breasted cock in the Brown-reds is as follows:—Head dusky brown; comb and face bright purple-red or smutty, according to taste; eyes black or dark brown; neck brassy, striped with black; the legs dark or willow; body-feathers dark brown—or even in a dark hen almost black, with brassy hackle, would answer for show.

This is the most fashionable color; let us now see what they will breed. Some will come as near like the parents as possible in cockerels; others will come black-breasted, and too dark in hackles; others will be near-ly crow-black, with only a dirty dark red on shoulder and back. Some pullets will come a nice color, but some nearly brown; and others nearly black, without the brassy hackle, but only a slight tinge of copper in the hackle. In Brown-reds it is very difficult to get above one or two in a brood fit for show, or even fit to breed from the following season; in fact, nothing we get in the Game line breeds so true to color as the Black-red, which is easiest to breed of all the varieties.

Another very fashionable color in Brown-reds, as frequently shown, and by many thought even more beautiful than the starling-breasted, is as follows:—Head and hackle orange-color throughout, with little or no streak in the feathers; shoulder-coverts a shade lighter crimson than the streaky-breasted birds; saddle to match the hackle, or dark lemon; back a maroon straw; and breast an almost black ground-color, but every feather beautifully laced with light bay—a mere slight lacing round the edges, not at all running into the feather. The hens to match these cocks are a brilliant black, with rich golden-striped hackle. The feathers of the cock are of great beauty. The accuracy with which the back and saddle feathers are striped in good birds is remarkable.

From this we will go to the brick-breasted, which is the nearest approach to the laced-breasted Brown-reds. The cock is a similar color in back to the last, but a little more crimson on shoulder and less orange in the hackle; and in general, lighter in color on the saddle, more a shade of orange prevading all over the body; black or brown eyes in general, and red in the face. By crossing this color with a pure black-bodied hen, you would get a portion of streaky-breasted cockerels, but few dark pullets, most of the pullets running light browns; but being very pretty and slightly pencilled, they are much admired, and make very good mates for ginger Brown-red cocks, their colors seeming to harmonize well. The ginger Brown-red cock is a most beautiful bird; head and hackle-feathers being a dark lemon; back and shoulders a blueish red, slightly crimsoned; breast a dun buff, mottled; and tail jet-black.

DUCKWINGED GAME.

The Duckwing is one of our most beautiful breeds of Game; the bright gay colors are so beautifully blended together that no one, not even a non-breeder, fails to admire this splendid bird. His face is well-defined crimson; the head just covered with silver-white, small, fine feathers; hackle almost white, only a tinge of straw pervading; his back a maroon straw and claret; saddle just a shade darker than the hackle, the feathers being very fine and short, just long enough to hide the points of the wings. The shoulders are a nice brass or brassy maroon right from the butts to the clear steel bar, and no light streaks, which will however appear, if not very carefully bred, just about one inch from where the brass-color begins from the butts; the shoulder-butts themselves black; breast black; tail black, with a shade of bronze pervading the sickles; eyes red, legs willow or yellow; weight from five to six pounds.

The hen to match should have the head grey; comb and face bright red; hackle silver-grey, darkly striped; breast a bright salmon-red; back and shoulder-coverts ought to be a slaty-grey, free from any ruddiness or pencilling. The tail a dark grey, almost black; inside fluff a steel-grey; legs willow or yellow.

To breed Duckwing cocks and hens, and to get rich colors you must have a cross from the Black-red each way. Sometimes you may get them by breeding together, but rarely cocks; hens you can. It is always best to put a pure-bred Duckwing hen to a really fine, bright Black-red to get cocks; all our best birds are bred this way, and the purer-feathered Black-red the cock is, the brighter you get your Duckwing. In breeding for hens, either Duckwing cock or Duckwing hens put together, or a very hard, good partridge-colored Black-red hen, will bring what you want; but if you get too much Duckwing by itself you will have soft, mossy-feathered birds. The way to obviate this is every second year to breed a pure Duckwing hen or two, and put her to one of the clear Black-red cocks. The reason we see so few really good Duckwings, either in hens or cocks, is that it takes so great an amount of care in crossing to keep it any way up to the standard; but when got, there is nothing more beautiful in the Game fowl. It is bad for a novice to go too much into crossing, but he should buy the purest-feathered fowls he can get, and breed till he finds out a little by experience.

The Silver-grey Duckwing is a most handsome fowl, so is the Silver-grey hen to match.

What are termed Birchen Duckwings are merely birds bred from Duckwings on both sides, and sometimes will come from the cross of Brown-reds and Duckwings. This breed cannot be admired, for the simple reason that there is no purity of feather. The nearest description that can be given is as follows:—Head and hackle dark straw, mixed with rusty brown; breast, creamy brown, a "hodge-podge" color of cream and rusty brown straw; saddle, straw and rusty brown; wing-butts, dull brown; bow, copper-brown; coverts, mottled rusty brown and claret, with a dash of straw; tail black, slightly bronzed; legs willow or carp. Hen to match, a dirty dark grey, almost a brown—in fact, the Silver-grey hen in all points only browner, and a few distinguishing colors or markings, the shoulders being a little greyer than the back.

PILE GAME.

This is a breed very much admired, and always was. There are several varieties which merely vary in a few different colored feathers, such as the Worcester Piles and Cheshire Piles, having a few black feathers inter-mixed in body and tail; whereas the Lancashire Pile is of pure colors, being white where a Black-red is black, and such we will describe, although a slightly-marbled breast is highly prized if not too heavy: Symmetry a little lighter or more sprightly than a Black-red in general; head a chestnut-red; hackle running a little lighter in color than the head; face a brighter red, and the chestnut carried right to the point of the hackle. Back, chestnut and claret-color; shoul-der-coverts and bow of the wings a rich red violet; breast, higher part marbled, or each feather laced with a pale chest-nut, inclining to a shade of blue; wing-coverts white edged with red chestnut; the tail white or merely a slight tick of black in the sickles, both in great and small sickles; thighs white; under part of body white; eyes red; legs yellow, white, or willow.

The Pile Game hen's head is a light chestnut; hackle white, faced with yellow chestnut; the back a white ground-color, slightly laced with red, a shade of gold pre-vading; and salmon-colored wing-coverts almost similar to back, but just a little heavier in the dark color; breast a rich chestnut right up to the throat, running off to white but not pure on the thighs; tail almost a pure white; eyes red; legs yellow, white, or willow.

Piles breed true to color, but now and then a cross of the Black-red is thrown in to give hardness of feather; but destroy every Black-red produced from this cross, for when it gets about the country it is most mischievous in the Black-red blood to those who are deceived with it, taking all the rich bright colors away, and producing those soft, mossy, mealy-colored pullets and cockerels, with light reddish straw hackles and saddles, beside a softness of feather, which are sometimes seen.

WHITE GAME

Is a beautiful variety. When in a nice grass-run a whole flock looks well, but when kept in confined spaces, and they get their feathers soiled, the beauty is gone, only symmetry left; and it is strange to see how few really grand and symmetrical Whites you find, and fewer still with the closeness or hardness of feather that is desirable in Game fowls. Whites were always looked upon as delicate, and few came off victorious in the pit; so no care was taken of them to improve either hardness of feather or style, which has been done in other breeds. There is no doubt but they can be improved in both qualities, and there is really a good opening at present for any one to go into the White Game breeding. Select a really rich Red Game cock, as short and hard in feather as possible, to cross in with; kill all the Red chickens; select then a White cockerel from this cross, and put to the White hens had previously, and the White pullets from the cross to the pure White cocks. This is where Piles have gained so much on the Whites; by the benefit of the Black-red cross, the feather is shorter and harder; better symmetry and hardier constitution are got, and altogether a much better bird.

To describe the White Game fowl, the one word White would do—head and hackle pure white, body white (a least shade of yellow not a disqualification), tail pure white, breast white, legs yellow or white, eyes red. The White Game hen everywhere white, but eyes, comb and wattles, which are all coral red; and legs yellow or white. Of course the beak must match the legs.

BLACK GAME

Are not so greatly admired—only by the few that have

kept them for any purpose—although at one time they used to be kept for the pit in some districts, but not being found so quick and active as most breeds, they were discarded, although "game" to the death. The color is a most splendid black, of metallic brilliancy, shades of green and purple pervading the whole body, with coral-red face; the legs dark willow or black. The hen also a pure glossy black, with a red coral comb and wattles. A cross from a dark Brown-red hen would greatly improve this breed, both in style and hardness of feather, by acting on the same principle as on the White Game, killing all the Brown-reds and reserving nothing. but the Blacks.

HENNY GAME.

The Henny strain never breeds a long-tailed cock unless crossed. The contrary has been stated by many persons, but the mistake has arisen from various birds which have not been true-bred Henny, but only the product of some cross; such will, of course, breed both kinds of plumage, but the true-bred Henny never does.

On the whole, the probability is that the breed is descended from some very ancient progenitor, which accidentally exhibited the peculiar hen-plumage, and struck the fancy of its proprietor. In laced Bantams, which are known to have derived their hen-tailed character from a single cock which took Sir John Sebright's preference (and which was very probably itself descended from hen-tailed Game), we see how apt the feature is to transmit itself with a little care; and that our supposition is correct, and that the strain once formed was preserved sedulously apart from a period now impossible to determine, is rendered further probable by the different colors and style of birds, which are very different from the standard breeds of Game. In style they are larger and heavier, occasionally reaching as much as nine pounds, and approaching the kind of bird formerly bred by cock fighters much more than those now bred by fanciers. In color they vary greatly. There are also Blacks, Greys, and other colors, besides mixtures arising from crossing them. The Reds, and in fact, most other colors of Hennies, have white or pinky-white legs, and, of course, white skins. These points, with their large size, make them decidedly the best for table of any breed of Game; their hardiness being also a recommendation to those who only wish fowls for table purposes, but who share our own opinion that the Game fowl is the finest eating of all varieties of poultry.

CLAIBORNE GAME.

The Claibornes were formed, it is said, by crossing the English breed known as Lord Seftons (a Black-red) with Spanish-bred hens, and are remarkable for the hens almost always having long and sharp spurs, while the weapons of the cock are so keen that the birds are often fought naturally, instead of being armed with steel.

HEATHWOOD GAME.

This is a strain which have achieved much success in the pit of late years, bred by Thomas Heathwood and called after him. They are bred in all the usual colors showing great mixture of blood.

INDIAN GAME.

The birds known by the name of Gallus Bankiva in Devon, Cornwall, are undoubtedly bred from Indian importations, and present the Malay type in some points very strongly, being chiefly wanting in the peculiar "sharp" shoulders so characteristic of that breed. They are, however, harder in flesh as well as in feather, and some of them are of undoubted courage. These birds generally stand rather low, are agile and active, and have been known in India (and in Cornwall too) to stand up well occasionally against good English blood. They are the prevalent style of bird kept in the neighborhood of Bengal, and, indeed, more or less throughout the whole continent of India. Some of them are of great endurance, and such birds have been known to realize as much as 700 rupees; indeed, often no sum whatever will purchase them.

In Malay proper, where we might expect to find the Malay type more strongly marked, the most esteemed kind of Game cock is, on the contrary, of a quite distinct character, differing alike from both the Indian and English breeds of Game, and evidently partaking more of the character of the true jungle-fowls.

Malay fowls are found good in all colors, for they are nearly all Game, and no doubt spring largely from the jungle-fowl, which abounds in the Malay peninsula, and also in Sumatra.

Malays rarely if ever cut combs, and never the feathers. There is no comb peculiar; they are both tall and rose-shaped, though the best birds have generally high and single combs. [This shows plainly its distinctness from the "Malay" breed.]

Some birds live for years and win many matches, for generally one escapes altogether. The spurs vary in outline, some being straight, some curved, and some waved; but all have edges as sharp as razors, and are in fact like blades of penknives fastened on. This makes the fighting very quick. It takes yards and yards of soft cotton thread, wrapped round and round in all sorts of ways, to keep the spur firm *in loco;* and this is the first art of a Malay. The straight spur is generally fastened under the foot, close to the ground; the crooked spur in the natural position. They take a long time to heel the birds, and lots of people, (friends) look at the position, and give their advice. Many of the birds are carefully trained. The birds know their owners, and they handle them most dextrously.

The birds are generally put out of hand on the ground by the competitors at say eight or nine yards apart; but each man seeks to put his bird down at advantage, and there is manœuvring. The result depends much on training. Some run under and others fly high; it matters not how they meet, but meet they do, and strike home. They often meet together high up in the air. So keen are the edges of these deadly weapons, and so dreadful are the wounds, that generally one cock at once falls dead or next door to it, so that the other has only to give just one peck and rise, and it is over; but sometimes the dying bird lays hold of the unwounded one, and by a well-directed blow kills his assailant at once, and wins the battle. They are seldom touched after once let go, because one is *hors de combat.*

OTHER GAME.

These are about all the varieties usually exhibited, but we have many other local breeds, though nothing self-colored. There is Black with brassy wings, the hen to match; mostly bred from birds a dirty black with a blue shade. Also the Spangles, almost every other feather being red and white, and tail black and white; the hens to match this are nearly the color of a Houdan hen, only more broken in tint, and not inclined to spangle so evenly. The Furness Game are a smoky blue, with brass wings, and almost a black hackle; hens blue, speckled with black streaks, hackles dark, tail dark. Cuckoo Game is a very scarce variety, not much prized either for beauty of feather or style, being a smutty blue in body-color, with light markings all over; hackle a shade darker than body. This breed could be greatly improved with the cross of the short-feathered ginger Brown-reds. I think by picking the Brown-red to cross by with a shade of blue in him, there would not be so much chance of losing the cuckoo-markings as with any other cross.

The Tassel breed is so called from their having a tassel, or crest of long feathers, on the side of the head. The Muffs are birds having a lot of feathers about the throat. The Rose-combs are distinguished by having a low spiked comb. The Round-polls show clear indications of crossing with the Asiatic. These breeds do not require further mention, being only to be met with occasionally.

HINTS ON JUDGING GAME.

In judging Game, activity and liveliness are taken into consideration, as well as condition and other points. It is very seldom, however, that first impressions are wrong unless competition is very close. Many are "made up," just to stand the test of passing the judge on the required day, and after that they are out of form. In Game it is generally needful really to put the "points" together; and hens and cocks should be judged by the same scale.

In judging Game it is needful to be watchful against evident traces of the Malay cross. Without going into the question of whether such a cross may or may not in certain cases improve a strain, there can be no doubt that if it be employed it should be entirely "bred out" again before showing, and that no bird showing plain signs of it has any right to take a prize as true Game. That cross-bred birds exist, almost any class at a good show will testify for itself. A real Malay cross can generally be detected by the head being too broad, with rather heavy eyebrows, or the neck being too long, or, failing these, by a sort of undefined stiffness or awkwardness of gait, which is as distinct from the elastic tread of the Game as can well be.

SCHEDULE FOR JUDGING GAME.

GENERAL CHARACTERISTICS OF COCK.

Head and neck—General appearance of head rather long, thin and keen; beak strong, slightly curved, and stout where set on; whole face smooth and fine in texture, including deaf-ears and throat. (In undubbed birds the comb should be upright, thin, straight, and evenly serrated; deaf-ears and wattles also very thin, red and smooth in texture.) Eyebrows free from "lowering" expression, which denotes Malay blood. Neck somewhat long and slightly arched; hackle short, so as just to reach between the shoulders, but not to flow over the back. Body—General shape rather slight, largest at shoulders, and tapering to the tail somewhat like the shape of a fir-cone; back flat, widest at shoulders, and tapering towards saddle, and somewhat slanting; breast hard and full, but not deep or turkey-breasted; saddle narrow, the feathers short and scanty; wings powerful and of moderate length; the points nicely carried under the saddle-feathers. Legs and feet—Thighs rather long, but well carried along the body, not perpendicularly, or so as to appear long, very round and hard; shanks in just proportion, with smooth handsome scales, the spurs set on rather low; toes long, straight, and thin, with well-shaped nails, and the back toe low and nearly flat on the ground. Tail—A nice medium length, neither too close or too spread, but only moderately raised, and each sickle-feather as nearly as possible just clearing the next one and no more; the sickles and whole plumage sound, hard, and glossy. Size—Rather small, ranging from four pounds and a half to six pounds. General Appearance—Rather slim, but showing much agility, strength, "elasticity," and vigor, with great hardness of flesh and plumage. Carriage—Very upright, alert, and courageous.

GENERAL CHARACTERISTICS OF HEN.

In all respects similar to those of the cock, except that the tail is carried not much above the horizontal line, and her comb should be thin, upright, quite straight, and neatly serrated. Size—Rather small, averaging about four pounds and a half. General Appearance—Very neat and trim. Carriage—Alert, quick, and active.

VALUE OF POINTS.

General Symmetry............................ 20
Color...................................... 15
Handling (*i. e.*, Hardness and Condition)........ 15
Head....................................... 10
Eyes....................................... 10
Neck....................................... 5
Tail....................................... 10
Legs....................................... 5
Feet....................................... 10

100

STANDARD OF PERFECTION.—A bird pefect in shape, style, color, condition and hardness of body and feather, to count in points 100

VALUE OF DEFECTS.

DEFECTS TO BE DEDUCTED.

Bad head.............................. 10
Too much hackle............................. 7
Tail too long, or spread........................ 8
Legs (not in proportion)......................10
Imperfect feet...............................12
Eyes wrong color............................. 8
Other faults in color.........................15
Want of symmetry...........................22
Want of condition (as to appearance)..........12
Want of hardness (on handling).............. ...12

DISQUALIFICATIONS.—Crooked backs, crooked breasts, duck-feet, or any other evident weakness or deformity. Color of legs not matching in a pen. Any other than single combs. Adult cocks undubbed. Any fraudulent dyeing, dressing, or trimming, beyond the recognised dubbing and dressing of the head.

www.ingramcontent.com/pod-product-compliance
Lightning Source LLC
Chambersburg PA
CBHW020328090426
42735CB00009B/1446